Social Investigation in
Physical Education and Sport

Social Investigation in Physical Education and Sport

E D Saunders
School of Physical Education
Ulster College, The Northern Ireland Polytechnic
Newtownabbey, County Antrim

G B White
Carnegie School of Physical Education
City of Leeds and Carnegie College, Leeds

LEPUS BOOKS · LONDON

© 1977 Lepus Books
An associate company of Henry Kimpton Limited
7 Leighton Place, Leighton Road, London NW5 2QL

ISBN 0 86019 030 7

Computer Typesetting by Print Origination
Orrell Mount, Hawthorne Road, Bootle L20 6NS

Printed by Cambridge University Press, Cambridge

Contents

Preface

Recent years have seen a considerable expansion of the number of courses in colleges and university departments which focus upon the social aspects of teaching and learning. Two difficulties often face newcomers to this field. First, few text books, monographs or papers have been published which give authoritative and up-to-date accounts of matters of practical concern to specific subject areas in schools, such as physical education, home economics, drama or science. This book has been designed to overcome this problem by focussing upon topics of immediate importance to subject teachers, in particular, teachers of physical education. As many of the techniques which have been employed have been chosen for their application to a variety of situations, it is anticipated that they will also be useful to teachers and students who wish to study other subjects of the school curriculum. The second difficulty is equally persistent. No matter how much care is taken to provide a thorough analysis of social processes at work in the school and the community, traditional teaching methods including lectures, seminars and tutorials may not be the most effective way of capturing the interests or ensuring the involvement of students. To counter this difficulty the approach adopted in this book encourages maximum student participation by giving them primary responsibility for directing their own learning. This is achieved by means of a series of projects or self-instructional packages which can be carried out individually or in groups and give practice in ways of observing, describing and analysing social behaviour.
We hope that the topics covered in this book will prove attractive to students, teachers and tutors and to others who wish to know more about the relationship between sociology, sport and physical education.

E.D. SAUNDERS
G.B. WHITE

ACKNOWLEDGEMENTS

The authors wish to thank the Editor and publisher of the *Bulletin of Physical Education* for permission to reproduce the figure on p. 37 from an article by Crunden (1970), and The Controller of Her Majesty's Stationery Office for permission to reproduce the Tables on pp. 42 and 43 from Sillitoe (1969) "Planning for Leisure".

Part 1 # Introduction

THE PROFESSIONAL TRAINING OF TEACHERS OF PHYSICAL EDUCATION

The traditional approach to the professional training of teachers in physical education departments has been to assign a set number of students to a single methods tutor who, with the occasional assistance of other specialist members of staff, provides courses in physical education in which students are offered skills, knowledge and other appropriate educational experiences necessary for their future teaching roles. This expertise has been gained by first hand experience of handling groups of children in teaching situations in which tutors have learned to appreciate the qualitative differences between children, their aptitudes and attitudes, interests and antipathies and the multifarious considerations which make up the teaching day.

It is assumed by colleges which organize student learning on the group based principle that this is the most effective way of training teachers for their future professional roles. It is felt that in this way students are given some rough empirical insights into the process of social interaction in schools and are provided with guide lines for the selection of appropriate curriculum material and teaching methods. These sessions are normally accompanied by a series of lectures on aims and objectives in which general principles of physical education are examined in the light of contemporary educational thought.

Recently, however, physical educationists have realized that the increased complexity of teaching, the expansion of knowledge of the psychological and social processes at work in schools and in the community will demand a level of expertise and knowledge beyond the scope of any one tutor, and that professional judgements must be examined critically against a background of educational research provided by social science based disciplines. Consequently psychologists, social psychologists, sociologists, historians and philosophers now provide theoretical frameworks and research findings against which such matters as child development, pupil-teacher relationships and the influence of social factors upon pupil learning can be examined.

Unfortunately efforts to bring about a productive relationship between these social science based studies and the practical business of teaching have been thwarted by the inability of specialist course tutors to produce subject matter which is relevant to the immediate problems of teaching and learning. This situation has been exacerbated by the closed book attitude of some practitioners who deny the practicability of theories unless they conform closely to their own personal views. Practitioners are likely to be hostile to men who may, either directly or indirectly, challenge the bases of their professional judgements. Equally, theorists are distrustful of men of action who are unwilling to subject their commonsense explanations to the rigours of scientific analyses.

Sociology has not escaped this treatment. Because it deals with the things with which men are familiar and about which they possess some knowledge, sociology has been described as the science of the obvious which gathers detailed information about things everyone already knows. Moreover, the language of sociology which describes commonplace incidents and actions in an unfamiliar way creates antagonisms from practitioners who are naturally distrustful of those who cannot write or talk in a language which they understand. It is important to note that their complaint is rarely levelled at other areas of theory such as exercise physiology or biomechanics whose books and journals are frequently impenetrable to teachers of physical education. Perhaps the use of esoteric language is symptomatic of a new discipline asserting its right to academic respectability and in so doing jargon is overused for effect. We have made conscious efforts to avoid these pitfalls.

This book has been written in the belief that sociological perspectives, concepts and research findings provide an important set of intellectual tools to promote insights into such matters as the content of the curriculum of physical education and interpersonal relationships of pupils and teachers. It is also a guide for those who seek access to a more informed and systematic analysis of the complex relationship between education and sport in a variety of social settings.

Social Aspects of Physical Education and Sport

Three considerations were paramount in thinking about the social aspects of physical education and sport. First, it was realised that the scope of this book precluded an exhaustive analysis of this largely uncharted field of study. As a result the term the social aspects was preferred to the term sociology since the orientation of the text was introductory and aimed at clarifying problems in physical education and sport, not sociological problems as such. Nevertheless, the perspectives and techniques employed are based upon and intended to provide a working knowledge of sociology as a discipline. The reader starts with what is familiar and looks at this in an unfamiliar, sociological manner to give experience in the handling of sociological techniques and the evaluation of research findings which relate to sporting behaviour in school and community settings. Second, it was assumed that any event of human occurrence could be analysed from a variety of points of view and that sociology had no prior claim to be the discipline of most immediate relevance in coming to understand the social significance of sport or physical education. The whole range of social science disciplines are at the disposal of anyone who wishes to understand human society in a more systematic and scientific way. Third, a clear distinction was made between the empirical and theoretical studies of sociology and the normative orientation of physical educationists or recreationists who believe that the results of sociological investigations will lead to constructive social action. Perhaps the major difficulty in analysing the relationship between sociology, sport and physical education was to devise a frame of reference which would not be subject to a variety of interpretations or more likely misinterpretations. Few writers make a clear distinction between the Sociology of Sport and the Sociology of Physical Education and some with good reasons assume that one is the subset of the other. It may be helpful, therefore, to look more closely at these relationships.

Sports Sociology or the Sociology of Sport

From the simplest point of view no one would doubt that sport as a special type of game, which was defined by Loy as 'any form of playful competition whose outcome is determined by physical skill, strategy or chance employed singly or in combination' (Loy, 1969) is a fair description of the physical activities which form part of a programme of education, recreation or sport in schools, youth clubs and adult organizations. In this sense sport and physical education embrace a range of activities, the form and practice of which are culturally determined and demand the employment of physical skills and abilities and the demonstration of physical prowess. The educational, recreational and sports contexts, therefore, are social settings within which these activities can be analysed from a variety of points of view, sociological or otherwise. Subject matter from the biological and physical sciences, the behavioural and social sciences, historical and comparative study are at the disposal of anyone who wishes to examine sport in a more scientific and informed way.

The study of sport or physical education, therefore, consists of the development and application of a number of theoretical perspectives which are considered valuable in coming to understand sport in different contexts. Each has different conceptual structures and different forms of validation for its propositions. It is a field of activity around which many forms of knowledge may focus. Its unity comes from collections of knowledge from various forms which unite solely because they relate to sport. This was the sense in which Kenyon (1969) defined the work of the sports sociologist as one who:

> has the understanding of sport per se as his goal, albeit with the help of sociological theory and research.

Clearly this orientation differs from the activities of sociologists of sport who focus upon sport or physical education as fertile fields for sociological research providing unique laboratories in which to investigate central sociological questions. In their work they share a common concern with other sociologists who seek to refine perspectives on such matters as socialization and social control, patterns of social class and social mobility, or patterns of social change, albeit within the context of sport or physical education. We can anticipate, therefore, that sports sociologists direct their attention to gaps in sports theory, whilst the sociologist of sport is concerned with gaps in sociological theory. From a research perspective we can also anticipate that the sports sociologist, whilst adopting the specific orientation of the sociologist, will develop co-operative research strategies of an interdisciplinary nature to promote an understanding of sport as such. The sociologist of sport on the other hand will use sport as a means, not an end, and his research strategies will be determined by the need to develop sociological understanding. It is not beyond the scope of imagination, however, to anticipate that research could be formulated to examine problems of interest to students of social behaviour and to analyse questions of special interest to sports theorists. Moreover, because most of the work in the sociology of sport and sports sociology is undertaken in departments of physical education, it can be assumed that specialists will share a desire to facilitate two way traffic between the refinement and elaboration of their perspectives and the work of professional physical educationists and recreationists. Sociological understanding commends itself to anyone whose goals involve the manipulation of people, whatever their moral purpose, even if it is not always clear to them that there is nothing inherent in sociology that leads to practice. It is obvious, therefore, that sociologists, sports theorists and practitioners will adopt different perspectives. When we enter the field of education the conceptual distinctions between sports sociology and the sociology of sport and educational sociology and the sociology of education are clearly different (Saunders, 1973). Unlike sports sociology which is orientated to an understanding of sport as such, educational sociology goes beyond the understanding of education and is primarily concerned with the contribution that specialist studies such as sociology make to the practical activity of educating. This contrasts with the approach of sports sociology which is not undertaken with some practical purpose in mind.

Educational Sociology and the Sociology of Education

The fundamental difference between educational sociology and the sociology of education relates to the basic difference between educational and sociological enquiries. Educational theory is related to practice and is knowledge pursued to determine practical activities. Sociology, on the other hand, is directed towards:

> a body of interconnected propositions (hypotheses, generalizations) concerned with a particular problem area and meant to account for the empirical facts in it (Nadel, 1965).

The distinction between scientific theory and the theory of practical activities is the traditional distinction between knowledge that is organized for the pursuit of knowledge and the understanding of our experience, and knowledge that is organized for determining a practical activity (Hirst, 1966). The sociologist, therefore, is interested in education because it is one of the central activities of our society, whilst the educator is concerned with the contribution that sociology can make to the practical activity of educating and makes use of these findings or conducts research with a useful purpose of some kind in mind. The distinction is not absolute and in fact work can be constructed to contribute both to the growth of general sociological theory and to the solution of practical problems (Gross et al, 1958). However, the predominant approach of educational sociology which has enjoyed a great deal of popularity in the United States has tended to be:

> hortatory rather than empirical, inspirational rather than objective, and synoptic rather than analytic (Taylor, 1966).

Despite the plea that there is nothing inherent in sociology which leads to practice, the educational sociologist has made selective use of sociological findings to substantiate implicitly established goals and has covertly moved from the objective and scientific endeavour of sociology to the subjective and normative approach of the educationalist.

Kenyon and Loy clearly identified this orientation in the literature of physical education and sport in the U.S.A. and Europe where a clear distinction could be made between normative and non-normative sports sociology. Those who subscribed to the former approach assumed that the goals of physical education, sport or recreation were implicitly established, that considerable consensus existed to their nature, and sought hard evidence to convince others of these values. Non-normative sports sociology, on the other hand, was not governed by goals of social action or social improvement and did not seek to influence public opinion or behaviour nor to find support for implicitly established 'social development' goals as described in the writings of eminent physical educationists (Kenyon & Loy, 1969). By taking up such a position Kenyon and Loy did not suggest that physical education ought not to be value free and clearly indicated that the choice of both ends and means could be enhanced considerably by drawing from the findings of a well developed sports sociology.

The Question of Values in the Sociology of Sport and Physical Education

Many sociologists reject this idea of value freedom and maintain that it is impossible to keep values from entering sociological study. Values enter into the selection of problems and the interpretation of findings, if not into choice of methods and the collection of data. Even the selection of a particular pre-theoretical perspective for the analysis of sport or physical education will be based upon a particular model of the relationship between man and society.

Within sociology at least two distinctive pre-theoretical perspectives have emerged which differ in that one emphasizes man in SOCIETY whilst the other emphasizes MAN in society. In their crudest form they are known as the 'systems' and 'action' approaches and posit antithetical views of the relationship between man and society. The former, the systems approach, stresses the constraint that society exercises over the individual to ensure a measure of social order, whilst the latter, the action approach, stresses the role of the individual in constructing his own social world so that society as an entity is external to the individual yet depends upon the individual for its construction and maintenance. The reason for these emphases can be found in the historical setting in which sociology arose and the opposing problem of social order and individual control that had to be faced (Dawe, 1971).

Kenyon and Loy's (1969) definition of the sociology of sport as:

the study of social order—the underlying regularity of human social behaviour—

including efforts to attain it and departures from it within the context of sport emphasizes the constraint the social system exercises over the individual so that systems of concepts and general propositions derive their significance, their meaning and their relationship of interdependence from the notion of external constraint. In short, the notion of social order incorporates a social philosophy, that is a complex body of facts and judgements of value. This challenges the declaration of a value-free sports sociology.

It is doubtful whether any scientist is value free for the mere selection of a topic for investigation indicates a scale of values. Moreover, objectivity may be more easily attained by the natural scientist who studies how 'things' behave in the physical world than by the social scientist who studies people. The meanings which people attach to their actions is the subject of study of the social sciences and these cannot be readily quantified whereas the behaviour of natural phenomena can be understood as a necessary reaction to a stimulus which can be easily identified and quantified. Nevertheless, the detached sociologist will attempt to leave behind his own convictions and beliefs and attach great value to objectivity. He tries to control and understand his own values to eradicate as far as possible any prejudice or bias that may enter his work.

Sociology and Practice

The difficulty of remaining 'value-free' should not prevent the sociologist from acting as a consultant to practitioners whose primary concern is to find the most effective way of attaining their specific objectives. However, the client's concern for social improvement through sport, profit through the sale of sports goods or social development through physical education should not pressurise the sociologist into saying more than his findings permit as is implied by those who subscribe to a normative sports sociology. Sociologists should not invent, fabricate or apply evidence selectively to assure themselves of public acclaim, no matter how lofty the ideals of their employers and, in the end, the results of research may challenge the goals of the practitioner and lead to a redirection of courses of action.

In a recent review of educational research in Great Britain one writer (Hoyle, 1973), has noted that sociologists may also become involved in planned change through action research where the entire research strategy will be different from the approach of the detached research. He will relinquish traditional modes of verification to manipulate the situation in which he himself is involved. This approach implies that the sociologist cannot ignore the uses to which sociology might be put and that he has a moral commitment to be aware of the dangers which interference in the lives of people may bring. In the case of education which is at base a manipulation of people, teachers or children, such dangers are particularly strong. At this stage of development, however, we doubt whether any physical educationist is involved in this role.

We have attempted to clarify some of the differences between the sociology of sport, sport science or sports theory and sport sociology but no clear orientation has been given to the sociology of physical education or the physical education domain of educational sociology. Is it to be conceived as a sub-domain of the sociology of sport as suggested by Kenyon or does the rationale for the sociological study of physical education gain its major orientation and research impetus from a carefully formulated sociology of education? Before turning to the particular problem, it may be useful to consider contemporary developments in the uncertain relationship between sociology and physical education.

Sociology and Physical Education

It is only recently that sociologists or physical educationists with sociological training have committed themselves to the study of physical education and this heightened interest has led to a great deal of theorizing much of which has not been based upon the results of empirical research. Most empirical studies which have been conducted by sociologists here have been concerned with other aspects of school life and the spin off to physical education has been accidental rather than deliberate (e.g. Banks, 1955; Chetwynd, 1960; Ford, 1969; Gordon, 1957; Gross & Herriott, 1965; Hargreaves, 1967; Jackson & Marsden, 1966; Jackson, 1968; King, 1969; Lambert & Milham, 1974; Mays, 1965; Miller, 1961; Partridge, 1966; Shipman, 1968; Spinley, 1953;

Stevens, 1961; Taylor, 1953 and Waller, 1967). Despite this dismal record a number of surveys produced by physical educationists and sociologists have provided well documented and assiduously collated information on such matters as curricular and extra-curricular participation in physical education in grammar, secondary modern and technical schools. They have identified, for instance, changes in sporting preferences of different age groups in relation to sex and social class and the relationship between the objectives of teachers and the content of their programmes of physical activities (Abrams, 1966; Emmett, 1971; Kane, 1974; McIntosh, 1966; Saunders & Withering-ton, 1970; Sillitoe, 1969; Start, 1961; Start, 1967). One problem with data collected by survey techniques is that information as to causes is seldom explored. For example, a high correlation between sporting ability and scholastic achievement shows neither that sporting ability develops a greater desire to achieve academically nor that academic success will produce a talented athlete. It merely indicates that there is a relationship, not that one is the cause of the other. We are a long way from providing explanations of social behaviour within the context of school physical education. Perhaps there is a need to reconsider the methods we use to gather information upon which to build a viable theory of physical education.

The major problem for physical education, however, is that few sociologists are interested in the sociological study of physical education, whilst physical educationists have failed to give a clear orientation to the study of physical education which would provide the focus of sociological study. How can we account for this in a subject which has become increasingly committed to advancement in both research and writing? It is surprising that a profession which attaches so much importance to the necessity of developing good social relationships with students or children has seldom turned its attention to a discipline which purports to study these relationships. Frequently we hear of or read about the need to understand the relationship between physical education and social development and even the most sceptical teacher has at least considered its importance. Yet so few have felt the need to study these aspects objectively, to understand the nature of social relationships and to supplement personal experience by the findings from sociology. Perhaps the fault can be traced to colleges where judgments about teaching have been formulated from personal experience and any attempt to subject this experience to sociological analysis meets with resistance since it analyses what tutors already know to be true. When the sociologist ventures to question these truths he is accused of wasting time, or proving the obvious. Where he turns up inaccuracies or implausibilities he may be ignored, accused of inaccurate observation, or worst of all be berated as a 'theorist' for analysing a situation in which he has no experience. Men are distrustful of those who challenge self-evident truths.

More charitable observers would contend that the absence of a sociology of physical education can be traced to its later development as a sub-discipline so that physical education has by tradition based its knowledge upon the physical, biological and behavioural sciences. As a result, research endeavours have focused upon areas such as physiological, biomechanical and psychological aspects of skilled performance. Where these have focused upon the skilled behaviour of school age and school based children, they have proved a valuable source of information to the physical educator. These perspectives have proved attractive for at least two reasons. First, they focus upon the concreteness of human performance, that is action which can be readily identified, classified and analysed in laboratory situations. Second, the proliferation of research has produced a store of research techniques in contrast to the paucity of adequate research techniques in sociology. In this case the self-fulfilling prophecy prevails and researchers are attracted to areas of study where research techniques are readily available and in so doing promote one area of research over another. Moreover, the abstract nature of the sociological research seems to contrast with the concrete nature of studies in, for example, biomechanics, so that sociology which deals with the collective features of social life with the norms and values prevalent in groups which nevertheless become concrete only in the minds and actions of individual persons, has not become a major attraction to research bound physical educationists.

The reasons obscure one key factor—the development of the sociology of physical education will require a specific package of skills and knowledge and a willingness to apply them to the study of physical education. There is no doubt that the introduction of academic courses at degree and post degree level which are closely tied up with career developments, higher salaries and increased prestige has given a shot in the arm to developments in the sociology of physical education since most studies have focused upon problems in education not sport. Yet we should be able to look to the sociologist of education for some guidance, for some indication of the specific orientation of a sociology of physical education.

Sociology and Education

Unfortunately few sociologists of education have taken an active interest in the study of Physical Education. This is partly due to the shortage of sociologists who seek appointments in colleges, universities and polytechnics. It may also be traced to a feeling amongst sociologists that the study of physical education is a concern with the trivial and insignificant and is unlikely to attract graduates in a discipline whose own parentage is still suspect. It has also been encouraged by the tradition of sociology which has devoted its attention to the study of the relationship between educational success and failure and patterns of social stratification in which education has been defined narrowly as an individual's capacity to achieve academic success so that the study of 'non-academic' subjects has received scant attention (e.g. Banks, 1968; Floud, 1950; Floud et al, 1956; Glass, 1954; Halsey et al, 1961).

In broad terms, the dominant tradition of the sociology or education has stemmed from two distinct sources. The first, which has been dominated by social enquiry and documentation, has focused upon the relationship between educational opportunity and patterns of social stratification and social mobility and has consistently demonstrated that children from middle-class rather than working-class backgrounds reap the rewards of our educational system. More recently, the demand for people trained in technical, scientific, and administrative skills has become paramount and sociologists have been involved in the study of the wastage of human resources due to the inadequate distribution of educational opportunities. Sociologists, therefore, have been interested in education to understand some of the inequalities and social injustices associated with the provision of educational opportunities together with a sustained attention to the relationship of this provision to the national economy. Many of these studies have focused upon a child's opportunity to gain 'work-tickets' or qualifications for higher education, so that education has been interpreted in its narrow sense in terms of its vocational or instrumental purposes. Despite the plea by one eminent sociologist (Floud, 1967) in the early 1960's that there was a need then to provide opportunities for a more constructive and creative use of leisure to offset the debilitating effects of a machine technology, sociologists of education have ignored the non-vocational linked areas of the school curriculum to identify the contribution or non-contribution of subjects like physical education to this area of education. This is only one example of a number of omissions in research activities at this level.

The second mainstream of sociological enquiry has focused upon the school as an organization or a social system and most of the work of a sociological nature has focused upon the school using the more specific approach of the sociological study of organizations (e.g. Bidwell, 1965; Corwin, 1967; Gross & Fishman, 1968; Lambert, 1967; Musgrave, 1968; Shipman, 1968; Swift, 1969 and Silverman, 1971). Empirical work has primarily focused upon differentiation patterns in schools especially the grouping of pupils by ability in streams. These studies follow the mould of the earlier correlation studies which focused upon the relationship between educational opportunity and social class, except that they emphasise school based rather than community and societal based patterns of differentiation and stratification. They have provided useful insights into aspects of physical education in schools, in particular the function of physical education as a means of reducing patterns of differentiation associated with systems of streaming. These studies are superior to the earlier demographic studies of education in that some emphasis has been given to specific subject areas of the school curriculum even though these have been considered subsidiary in understanding cultural processes at work in schools.

During the last decade a third trend has become apparent in the sociology of education in which the emphasis has shifted from the organisational structure of the school to an emphasis on what is being taught. This change stems from three distinct sources: the first from an increased interest in the sociology of knowledge; the second from the Schools Council's work in curricular development; and the third from the theoretical orientation and influence of the Open University Course unit School and Society (for an overview of the state of contemporary approaches, see Bernstein, 1972). As a result the curriculum of schools is brought into sharp focus, pedagogical arrangements are examined and forms of assessment are critically appraised. Moreover, techniques of enquiry have moved from the social survey of large samples of the population by means of questionnaires to participant observation and case studies to provide close ethnographic descriptions of what happens in schools.

In this approach the knowledge properties of schools are not taken for granted but treated as problematic. Knowledge in its sociological connotation refers to organised experience, to all forms of thought and action used by individuals as a basis of social life. It does not simply refer to academic knowledge or forms of thought conceived as cerebral or high status; it also refers to commonsense or everyday knowledge which governs the behaviour of pupils and teachers. In particular, this approach brings into sharp focus the stratification of knowledge and its significance for the structuring of experiences of young people in our present day society. This can lead to the examination of particular educational ideologies which uphold a curriculum which is highly theoretical, abstract and unrelated to everyday life and conceived as high status in contrast to the curricula of practical subjects such as physical education which are low status, yet closely related to everyday life.

But what is the proper orientation of the sociology of physical education? If the system is studied either as an institution or as an organisation it has much in common with the orientation of the sociology of sport which is as much about stratification and mobility and organisation as it is about sport itself. In this sense, the sociology of physical education is a sub-domain of the sociology of sport. Because education is much concerned with moulding the realities of young people, one can argue that whereas studies of sport are contributory factors in the study of physical education, they are not central. Furthermore, it has been noted (Cohen, 1971) that:

> all educational systems have at least two pairs of function; first they communicate cultures or sub-cultures which exist and which will, at least, still continue to exist, thereby reinforcing social systems and sub-systems. However, in addition they also promote innovatory tendencies which mean they must provide both the skills and motivations to change at least some parts of cultural and social systems or add to them.

The study of physical education as culture (Lawton, 1975), therefore, is central to the study: values, norms, skills and knowledge will be the major concerns of sociologists of physical education. Using Loy's characterisation of sport and the present writers' definition of physical education, and obviously the two activities have many features in common, the physical education component of educational sociology can be described as the study of the conditions in which physical activity, characterised by physical skill, strategy or chance employed singly or in combination, contributes to the induction of children into membership of society. Possible developments in this field have been noted by at least one eminent sociologist who wrote 'we have in education a remarkable opportunity to study changes in the form of socialisation which control the body as a message system. From this point of view the transformation over the past decade or so of physical training into physical education and movement is of some interest' (Bernstein, 1972).

Techniques of Social Investigation in Physical Education and Sport

It must be made clear from the projects which follow that they range widely in perspective and no attempt has been made to describe or analyse the whole field of the sociology of physical education or sport as sub-domains of the sociology of education or the sociology of sport. The modest intention of the book is to introduce sociological perspectives, concepts, research findings and research techniques which provide some theoretical insights into the social processes at work primarily in schools and to give experience in the application of these to the development of a practical understanding of the relationship between this body of theory and selected practical situations. (Some aspects of the relationships between theory and practice are examined in Hirst, 1966 and Saunders, 1974.) Relevance and involvement are the keynotes of the text.

This is achieved by means of a series of projects, each of which is designed to be a viable unit of study which can be carried out individually or in small groups. These have been ordered to develop a knowledge of sociological perspectives, to give practice in the analysis of documentary evidence, to promote experience of observing and recording behaviour, to provide knowledge and skill in interviewing techniques and to study behaviour of groups in experimental situations. Although some projects will require a head count, it should be emphasized that it is not the heads, but what is in them, that counts. Nevertheless, the authors have deliberately included some fundamental statistical techniques which require only an elementary knowledge of figures. In fact, a number of studies require qualitative rather than quantitative analysis.

The selection of the projects is in a sense arbitrary and the principles we have employed could be easily adapted to illuminate the relationship between theory and practice in other areas of the sociology of physical education and sport. Each examines one aspect of practice from the viewpoints of both sociology and physical education and a clear distinction is made between careful description and analysis on the one hand and evaluation on the other. Deliberate attempts have been made to separate the former from the latter. Given a particular situation, the reader is asked to recognize the sociological factors at work, examine them systematically and critically and having done this carefully and painstakingly discern how they affect educational practice. In this way, sociology can be seen to contribute to the theory of physical education by providing basic understandings upon which rationally justified principles of practice can be based. Because a simple differentiation is made between the normative orientation of the educationist who utilises knowledge to determine what should happen in practice and the non-normative orientation of the social scientist who has the understanding of sport in schools as his goal, the book, by directing attention to areas of activity seldom explored by students of social behaviour may be of some interest and value to sociologists of sport.

The Projects

Within the broad view of sociology two distinct models of society have emerged which differ in the emphasis placed on the relationship between man and society. These are known as the 'systems' and 'action' models and in broad terms each governs the way in which we come to analyse the social life of schools. The former, the systems model, views education as a means of inducting children into what is permanently worthwhile in society and emphasizes the key role of teachers as agents of socialization and social control to achieve this purpose. The latter, the action approach, stresses the role of the individual in constructing his own social world so that the outcome of education is neither pre-determined nor pre-ordained; it is a matter of negotiation between teacher and taught. These, and related problems, are outlined in the first two projects.

In the next two, attention is drawn to the usefulness of social surveys in the formulation of programmes of physical education. The third project requires the secondary analysis of a single case study survey of a comprehensive school and the fourth project entails the examination of part of a large scale survey of sporting behaviour. Considerable attention is devoted to the difficulties of interpretation faced by the teacher who attempts to make valid generalizations from the results of these surveys. Other types of written and spoken communications, including the content of books, periodicals, newspapers and reports on radio and television, are often absorbed into the thought processes without any attempt being made to analyse the credibility of the information received. These forms of communication can be analysed systematically by a procedure known as content analysis. This technique is used in the fifth project to study differences in types of sports coverage within and between newspapers.

From this point we move to the observation and analysis of group behaviour to understand their formation, structures, processes and functional problems. The sixth project is concerned with the systematic observation of the recreational use of sports facilities to demonstrate that the usefulness and reliability of any body of information depends upon the accuracy with which it is observed and recorded. The seventh project establishes that sociometric analysis is a useful tool to discover friendship and other association patterns in school-based groups, for example, gymnastics or games, while the eighth project describes the relationship between verbal and non-verbal interaction and patterns of play in a team game.

The ninth and tenth projects offer practice and experience in the handling of questionnaires. The former utilizes data collection from a focused interview of teachers to ascertain the influence of tradition upon programmes of physical education in different types of school. The latter entails the administration of an attitude inventory given to children in schools to measure differences in attitude to physical education between boys and girls of different ages. Each project tests hypotheses derived from reviews of literature to show the importance of devising empirical enquiries within a theoretically relevant framework.

The last two projects turn to the study of behaviour in experimental situations. The major task of the eleventh project is to observe and record the effects of three styles of leadership upon patterns of teacher/pupil relationships in a physical education class to illustrate that learning outcomes and teaching styles are closely inter-related. The study and observation of the effects of competition, conflict and co-operation in small group activities is the subject of the final project. Conditions are generated artificially in a competitive team game to create intra-group competition and conflict, and the effects of these factors on individual and team performances are assessed.

Finally, although this book may make some contribution to the study of physical education, it has limitations. It has not been designed as a researcher's manual, nor does it set out to describe or analyse the whole field of the sociology of physical education. Scientific research will require a more thorough and comprehensive grasp of these and other techniques, whilst the elaboration of a substantive body of knowledge is also outside the scope of this book.

Our practice has been to select books or articles which give a superficial acquaintance of issues and problems related to each project. Those who wish to gain a more informed, intensive and systematic grasp of the social aspects of physical education and sport are advised to consult the references at the end of the book. It may well be, that with the steady increase in the volume of published material readers will find it more practicable to keep their own annotated bibliographies.

Bibliography

ABRAMS, M. (1966). Testing consumer demand in sport. *Sport & Recreation*. 7, 32-36.

BANKS, O. (1955). "Parity and Prestige in English Secondary Education". London: Routledge and Kegan Paul.

BANKS, O. (1968). "The Sociology of Education". London: Batsford.

BERNSTEIN, B. (1972). Sociology and the sociology of education: some aspects. In "School and Society Unit 17". Bletchley: The Open University Press. 99-109.

BIDWELL, C.E. (1965). The school as a formal organisation. In J.G. March. (Ed.). "Handbook of Organisations". Chicago: Rand McNally.

CHETWYND, H.R. (1960). "Comprehensive School". London: Routledge and Kegan Paul.

COHEN, P.S. (1971). Foreword. In, E. Hopper. (Ed.). "Readings in the Theory of Educational Systems". London: Hutchinson. 11-12.

CORWIN, R.G. (1967). Education and the Sociology of Complex Organisations. In D.A. Hansen and J.E. Gerstl. (Eds.). "On Education: Sociological Perspectives". London: Wiley.

DAWE, E.A. (1971). The two sociologies. In K. Thompson & J. Tunstall. (Eds.) "Sociological Perspectives". Harmondsworth: Penguin.

EMMETT, J. (1971). "Youth and Leisure in an Urban Sprawl". Manchester: University Press.

FLOUD, J. (1950). Educational opportunity and social mobility. London: The Yearbook of Education.

FLOUD, J., HALSEY, A.H., & MARTIN, I. (1956). "Social Class and Educational Opportunity". London: Heinemann.

FLOUD, J. (1967). The sociology of education. In A.T. Welford, M. Argyle, D.V. Glass & J.N. Morris. (Eds.). "Society: Problems and Methods of Study". London: Routledge and Kegan Paul. 528.

FORD, J. (1969). "Social Class and the Comprehensive School". London: Routledge and Kegan Paul.

GLASS, D.V. (Ed.). (1954). "Social Mobility in Britain". London: Routledge and Kegan Paul.

GORDON, C.W. (1957). "The Social System of the High School". New York: The Free Press.

GROSS, N., MASON, W.S. & MCEACHEARN, A.W. (1958). "Explorations in Role Analyses". London: Wiley.

GROSS, N. & HERRIOTT, R.W. (1965). "Staff Leadership in Public Schools". London: Wiley.

GROSS, N. & FISHMAN, J.A. (1968). The Management of Educational Establishments. In P.F. Lazarsfeld. (Ed.). "The Uses of Sociology". London: Weidenfeld and Nicolson.

HALSEY, A.H., FLOUD, J. & ANDERSON, C.A. (1961). "Education, Economy and Society". London: Collier-Macmillan.

HARGREAVES, D.H. (1967). "Social Relations in a Secondary School". London: Routledge and Kegan Paul.

HIRST, P.H. (1966). Educational Theory. In J.W. Tibble. (Ed.). "The Study of Education". London: Routledge and Kegan Paul.

HOYLE, E. (1973). The study of schools as organisations. In H.J. Butcher & H.B. Pont. (Eds.). "Educational Research in Britain". London: University Press. 39.

JACKSON, B. & MARSDEN, D. (1966). "Education and the Working Class". London: Routledge and Kegan Paul.

JACKSON, P.W. (1968). "Life in Classrooms". London: Holt, Rinehart and Winston.

KANE, J.E. (1974). "Physical Education in Secondary Schools". London: Macmillan.

KENYON, G.S. & LOY, J.W. (1969). Toward a sociology of sport. In J.W. Loy & G.S. Kenyon. (Eds.). "Sport, Culture and Society". London: Collier Macmillan. 37-38.

KENYON, G.S. (1969). A sociology of sport: on becoming a sub-discipline. In R. Brown & B.J. Cratty. (Eds.). "New Perspectives of Man in Action". New Jersey: Prentice-Hall.

KING, R. (1969). "Values and Involvement in a Grammar School". London: Routledge and Kegan Paul.

LAMBERT, R. (1967). The public schools: a sociological introduction. In G. Kalton. "The Public Schools: A Factual Survey". London: Longmans.

LAMBERT, R. & MILLHAM, S. (1974). "The Hothouse Society". Harmondsworth: Pelican.

LAWTON, D. (1975). "Class, Culture and the Curriculum". London: Routledge and Kegan Paul.

LOY, J.W. (1969). The nature of sport: a definitional effort. In J.W. Loy & G.S. Kenyon. (Eds.). "Sport, Culture and Society". London: Collier Macmillan. 56.

MAYS, J.B. (1965). "Education and the Urban Child". Liverpool: University Press.

MCINTOSH, P.C. (1966). Mental ability and success in sport. *Res. in Phys. Educ.*, I, 20-27.

MILLER, T.W.G. (1961). "Values in the Comprehensive School". Edinburgh: Oliver and Boyd.

MUSGRAVE, P.W. (1968). "The School as an Organisation". London: Macmillan.

NADEL, S.F. (1965). "The Theory of Social Structure". London: Cohen and West. 1.

PARTRIDGE, J. (1966). "Life in a Secondary Modern School". Harmondsworth: Penguin.

SAUNDERS, E.D. (1973). Sociological orientation to the study of physical education. In J.A. Mangan. (Ed.). "Physical Education and Sport: Sociological and Cultural Perspectives". Oxford: Blackwell. 10.

SAUNDERS, E.D. (1974). Theory and practice in physical education. *Bull. of Phys. Educ.*, 10, 13-21.

SAUNDERS, E.D. & WITHERINGTON, K.S. (1970). Extra-curricular activities in Secondary Schools. *B.J. Phys. Educ.*, 1, 10-14.

SHIPMAN, M.D. (1968). "Sociology of the School". London: Longmans.

SILLITOE, K.K. (1969). "Planning for Leisure". London: H.M.S.O.

SILVERMAN, D. (1971). "The Theory of Organisation". London: Heinemann.

SPINLEY, B.W. (1953). "The Deprived and the Privileged". London: Routledge and Kegan Paul.

START, K.B. (1961). The relationship between games performance of the grammar school boy and his intelligence and streaming. *B.J. Educ. Psychol.*, 31, 208-211.

START, K.B. (1967). Substitution of games performance as a means of achieving status amongst secondary schoolboys. *B.J. Sociol.*, 17, 300-305.

STEVENS, F. (1961). "The Living Tradition". London: Hutchinson.

SWIFT, D.F. (1969). "The Sociology of Education". London: Routledge and Kegan Paul. 191.

TAYLOR, W. (1953). "The Secondary Modern School". London: Faber.

TAYLOR, W. (1966). The sociology of education. In J.W. Tibble (ed.). "The Study of Education". London: Routledge and Kegan Paul.

WALLER, W. (1967). "The Sociology of Teaching". New York: Wiley.

Part 2   Sociological
          Perspectives

Project 1

SOCIOLOGY, THE SCHOOL SYSTEM AND PHYSICAL EDUCATION

Aims: 1. To develop some facility in using sociological ideas, concepts and research findings.
2. To show how the ideas and experience of teachers influence their models of reality.

Introduction

The initial problem in understanding the relationship between sociology and physical education is to appreciate that each area of study has adopted different theoretical perspectives, different concepts, and different methods of validating its propositions.

Sociologists by definition select and abstract only sociological variables for study, whilst physical educationists must consider all the multi-dimensional forces which affect their roles as teachers. The fact that sociologists have discovered that the social background of a home has a profound effect upon a child's attitude to physical education is only useful when it is seen against the backcloth of other factors which influence the day-to-day running of the physical education class. Children's attitude to physical education will influence their receptivity to the efforts of teachers to provide fruitful educational experience, as will the teacher's personality, his knowledge of his subject, hours devoted to physical education and provision of facilities. What to teach which category of child is therefore based upon the relative importance of many factors, and judgements are compounded of guesswork, hunches and speculation, as well as the results of educational research. Sociology, therefore, provides information of a specialized type and its usefulness will depend upon its relevance to the teacher's immediate problems and tasks.

Although sociologists are not indifferent to what happens in schools, they must remain objective when carrying out their research. They make a clear distinction between 'is' and 'ought', between fact and value, and attempt to remain neutral in their analyses of the social life of schools, to avoid making biased judgements which will affect the results of their studies. Sociologists who describe and develop theories about the social life of a school do not attempt to prescribe what should happen in practice. That is the business and central concern of the physical educationist. In practice, however, the attempt to remain value free cannot be fully achieved for the mere selection of a particular problem for study indicates a scale of values. Moreover, the theoretical perspectives adopted by sociologists may derive their meaning from a particular view of human nature and the relationship between the individual and society.

Within the broad view of sociology two distinct perspectives have emerged which differ in the emphasis placed upon the relationship between man and society—these are known as the 'systems' and 'action' approaches. The systems approach emphasises the constraints which society exercises over the individual whilst the action approach stresses the role an individual plays in constructing his own social world. The systems and action approaches therefore reflect conflicting interpretations of the relationship between man and society, interpretations which are rooted in contrasting sets of values. Put simply one places emphasis upon man in SOCIETY whilst the other shifts the emphasis to MAN in society [1].

It is possible to analyse physical education from either point of view and the following is an examination of the systems approach. This perspective is based on the assumption that there is a common core of values in society which determines human behaviour, and that the primary function of physical education is to ensure that each generation of children is educated into what is permanently worthwhile or valuable in society. This central core of values is the ultimate source of moral authority for the teacher which sets him over and above children and gives him the right to impose a common meaning or order on them. The notion of order presupposes that children cannot, of their own volition, create and maintain order so that external constraints are necessary to ensure social control. Without external controls and an extended period of socialization in schools social and moral disintegration would inevitably occur. As an agency of socialization [2] therefore physical education ensures that the individual acquires the many physical, social and moral qualities demanded of him by the society in which he will eventually function.

Study Area and Procedure

College tutors, teachers and students build up their models of the realities of teaching from the results of observations, imitation and practical experience. These models are subjective, often unconsciously adopted and seldom subjected to rigorous analysis. Some conservatives argue strongly that teaching is an art form, highly subjective and personal, and by definition not amenable to scientific analysis. Others adopt a more progressive approach and contend that since teaching takes place in a social context it lends itself to sociological observation and analysis. Unfortunately, attempts to examine the complexities of the teaching situation from this viewpoint can become sadly unstuck where the teacher has an imperfect understanding of the sociological enterprise. Some of these misunderstandings are outlined in the passage below.

'Fosbury Flop' Secondary Modern School

Fosbury Flop Secondary Modern School lies in the north-east corner of England in a catchment area in which there is an over-representation of lower socio-economic groups in comparison with the national average. The school was built as part of the local council's redevelopment scheme and shows little ingenuity in design or lavishness in the provision of facilities. A depressingly small gymnasium and assembly hall is shared by the school population of some five hundred boys and girls and there are no playing fields.

Most of the houses which surround the school are owned by the local council and occupied by underprivileged and deprived, unskilled workers. The professional people who work in the town prefer to live on the outskirts in privately owned homes, sending their children to private or local grammar schools—a process which, they envisage, will pass on their achieved status to their offspring. Therefore, the school population is drawn predominantly from the lower class district whose cultural attainments do not extend beyond the local betting shops and football club, bingo, and local pubs which seem to prevail in the area. The smoke and grime complete this picture of dismal desolation which is fairly typical of the slum schools portrayed so graphically in the 'Newsom Report'.

Most of the teachers live in the residential suburbs where poverty and dreariness are less evident. Their attitudes and values are middle-class conservative and provide a direct contrast to those of the majority of the pupils. The children are taught by a male and a female specialist teacher of physical education, both of whom have lost touch with modern developments in their subject, an indifference which is reflected in their approach to teaching children.

The school itself has few commendable features. The headmaster has adopted an authoritarian approach to teachers and pupils alike, a style of leadership which would be more appropriate to a totalitarian regime than a democratic institution. He is convinced that as the formal leader it is his primary task to ensure complete conformity from the pupils and where his rule is violated his threats of punishment are swiftly carried out. This legitimizes his authority and directs the behaviour of pupils into socially approved channels. His positional authority over teachers ensures that his coercive methods are adopted in the classroom; or so it would appear from my impressions. With few exceptions his decisions are given full support by the staff for a variety of reasons varying from bored indifference to enlightened self-interest. The physical education staff are no exception. They conceive of the good pupil as one who conforms to the norms of good conduct laid down by the school. The movement approach to physical education is, as yet, unheralded in the curriculum of the school, I suppose because an overemphasis upon individuality and self-expression could lead to problems and difficulties of social control.

The compulsory nature of physical education not only affirms and reinforces the power of the teacher, it also results in little satisfaction amongst their pupil subordinates who rebel in the sense that they give little support to extra-curricular, non-compulsory inter-school games. This produces a mutually hostile role relationship between teacher and pupil. However, not all pupils react in this way. The high academic streams are school orientated, work hard, wear school uniform, and do not indulge in officially proscribed school behaviour such as smoking, playing billiards, betting or visiting cafes, and consequently they receive favourable recognition from the school staff. They represent the school in inter-school matches reflecting not only a set of school values but also a set of values which are alien to their home background. On the other hand, the lower stream boys have developed negative attitudes to the school, are indifferent to the demands of the teachers, and have developed a mild form of delinquency, including law violation, a desire for thrills, toughness and disobedience, which is generated through their lower class social affiliations. Girls in the same social stratum are preoccupied with dress, personal appearance and their attractiveness to the opposite sex.

Since it is often stated that physical activities appeal to the 'physical' nature of adolescent lower streamed children and 'cerebral' activities to the higher streamed academically more able, it could be assumed that physical education should appeal to the lower streamed children, partly as a result of their inherent nature and partly as a means of compensating for their lack of achievement in academic studies. This is not so. One senses that their alienation from school is total and includes the rejection of the school's right to involve them in activities more suited to their needs and interests. Even where a pupil manifests an interest in sport, he prefers to pursue this out of school. This is typified by one boy, an excellent soccer player, who, when asked to represent the school, invented a story about looking after younger brothers and sisters after school to conceal the fact that he played for a local soccer team.

There is no doubt that the school is not achieving its educational goals. Many pupils are not involved in the school and many actively reject and violate school rules. Little self-determination is allowed in the selection of activities in the school and even in physical education, where a wide range of activities is common-place in other schools, this school still pursues a narrow curriculum. The children should be allowed a higher degree of autonomy to offset the teacher domination, to develop individuality and self-expression as a counter to the dullness of their limited existence. Even amongst the more physically and intellectually able pupils there is a lack of opportunity to pursue physical activities which offer individual choice, in the gymnasium, on the playing field, or in any other context in which physical activities take place. This affects girls more than boys. All children have a right to this type of education irrespective of home background, social class, intellectual or physical ability. Furthermore, teachers need to re-evaluate their official role to reduce their conflict with the children. Pupils should not be categorized according to a preconceived notion of the 'good' pupil role, especially when this favours the child with middle-class values. Under these circumstances the self-fulfilling prophecy comes into action, the good pupils become better, and the poor become worse. Teachers should realize that they embody a culture which is conservative and middle-class and in conflict with the culture of working class children. Cultural contact will depend upon the realization of differences rather than their accentuation. This was the crux of the 1944 Education Act.

Exercises

1. List five sociological concepts used by the writer.
   Briefly define them[3].
2. Specify five words or phrases which have emotional overtones.
3. Where does the writer move from description to prescription?
4. Select three observations put forward by the author which describe conflicts in interpersonal relations and from a review of relevant literature furnish evidence which supports or rejects these observations[4].
5. Outline strategies which could be used to reduce conflict between teachers and taught to ensure that the school would reach its goals more effectively.

Notes and Bibliography

(1) An excellent analysis of these contrasting approaches to education can be found in
EVETTS, J. (1973). "The Sociology of Educational Ideas". London: Routledge and Kegan Paul. 128-141.

(2) This description of socialization follows closely to a definition offered by
PARSONS, T. (1969) The school class as a social system. In A.H. Halsey, J. Floud, & C.A. Anderson (Eds.). "Education, Economy and Society". London: Collier-Macmillan. 434-455.

(3) WORSLEY, P. (1970). "Introducing Sociology". Harmondsworth: Penguin Education.

(4) Examples of books which describe conflicts in interpersonal relations in secondary schools are outlined below.
BANKS, O. & FINLAYSON, D. (1973). "Success and Failure in the Secondary School". London: Methuen.
HARGREAVES, D.H. (1972). "Interpersonal Relations and Education". London: Routledge and Kegan Paul.
SHIPMAN, M.D. (1968). "Sociology of the School". London: Longmans.
WALLER, W. (1967). "The Sociology of Teaching". London: Wiley.

Project 2

SOCIAL INTERACTION IN A PHYSICAL EDUCATION CLASS

AIMS: 1. To develop further facility in using sociological ideas, concepts and research findings.
2. To demonstrate that models of reality not only influence but are influenced by the process of interaction between teacher and taught.

Introduction

In the previous project selected sociological concepts and research findings were used to provide an understanding of some of the social factors which influence teachers' efforts to supply children with worthwhile educational experience. One of the fundamental assumptions underlying the previous approach was that schools exist to socialize children into predetermined social roles which are prescribed by the larger society or social system into which they must eventually fit. By ensuring that children adhere to a common core of values, schools are important agencies of social control which promote some measure of order in society.

It is appropriate to consider some of the weaknesses of the 'systems' approach. By failing to define in detail what is meant by a common core of values, from which teachers derive acceptable patterns of pupil behaviour, we are never sure what teachers of physical education should be doing. Even where there is some degree of consensus amongst teachers about these patterns of behaviour it is doubtful whether these are a reflection of the values and standards held by all pupils. Another related problem is that even where schools are justifiably described as centres of conflict, the systems approach usually explains deviant behaviour as the result of poor communication, a breakdown in control, or an unavoidable conflict of personalities. It is assumed that the strains on the system are easily remedied by opening new channels of communication or adopting more severe measures to counteract recalcitrant behaviour so that conflict is perceived as a temporary lapse in the otherwise healthy functioning of the school. The problematic nature of the teaching situation is thus underestimated in this approach.

One way of overcoming these problems is not to assume that the actions of individuals can be understood in terms of officially prescribed patterns of behaviour or values handed down from above, but to understand action as an increasing attempt of people to exert some control over existing situations. This will lead to the examination, for instance, of how teachers and pupils define the teaching situation, the courses of action open to each, the processes of negotiation, mechanisms for resolving conflicts and the difficulties of control which emerge. This project, therefore, has adopted the 'action' perspective of the sociologist to demonstrate that teaching situations can be

31

understood as the product of action and interaction which are governed by teachers' and pupils' different modes of perceiving and reacting to each other in practical classes.

One of the crucial factors which emerges when we analyse teaching in this way is the realization that teachers and pupils come to physical education classes from substantially different social worlds. Even where teachers and children have similar social backgrounds attempts to exercise a strong influence over behaviour will be modified by the children's physical, emotional and mental immaturity. These factors indicate that we cannot complacently accept that the outcomes of teaching and learning can be taken for granted and we must examine the context in which learning takes place. It is patently untrue to assume that children are like puppets on a string, manipulated and controlled by a cadre of professionals whose professional training and adult authority brook no disobedience from children whose inferior position and immaturity leave them open to an all embracing adult imposed world. The fact that teachers mention control and discipline as the most common problem in school refutes this claim.[1] The problematic nature of teaching is outlined in the passage which follows.

Study Area and Procedure

It is axiomatic among teachers that the first few days of teaching are paramount in determining the success or failure of teacher/pupil relationships. In fact college training has always emphasized that to make good the teacher must establish himself as a dominant force in the gymnasium, playing field or elsewhere. 'Lay down rigid rules in the first instance' is a precept familiar to teachers in training. Unfortunately this concept of teaching is only one side of the coin. It fails to account for the underlying hostility which strict disciplinarians create amongst children; it underplays the difficulties of sustaining this kind of relationship in a subject which has enjoyment as one of its major objectives; and it emphasises teacher domination in a subject in which current ideologies reflect the teacher as a consultant, not a dictator. Moreover, experienced teachers know that, where teaching consists of making children learn, subordination may also be temporary and, through time, children search out weaknesses, exploit them, and devise strategies to win favours from the teacher. In so doing they redefine the teacher's jurisdiction over them. Teaching, therefore, is a complex form of interaction, the results of which are partly determined by the different expectations and experiences of teacher and taught and partly by the process of negotiation which is an integral part of the learning process. To highlight some of these points of view, you are asked to read the following extract from an episode in the life of a young teacher and answer the questions posed at the end.

The Diary of a Young Teacher
'I was a young, inexperienced teacher who had been in the post for a matter of a few weeks and had become demoralized and dejected by my lack of control over one particularly difficult class of fourteen year old boys. In the initial euphoria of becoming a 'real' teacher I had unwisely ignored the friendly advice of other teachers in the school to treat this particular class firmly and punish indiscretions swiftly and

impersonally. Naturally I wanted to make good in the school, partly because this was expected of me and partly to secure my future career. Unfortunately, my desire to win over this class by friendly means and to prove to myself, and others, my superior teaching skill was a disastrous mistake. The fundamental problem was that I had lost control and unless I exerted some authority over the next few weeks I would not survive to the end of the term. It was crystal clear that I had to spare myself no unpleasantness in order to establish and secure my dominance.

The situation came to a head one Monday morning when I arrived to find the changing rooms in chaos. There was no immediate response to my shout for silence. Angrily I shouted at the top of my voice. Slowly it dawned upon the class that I was demanding their attention. After some scuffling, shuffling of feet and subdued muttering the class quietened down. 'Now, listen to me', I said; 'there are several people here who don't seem to be here to work. I'd sooner they didn't come to this class and I dare say they will be lucky to remain in the school.' Malevolently, I fixed my eye on one large youth, the principal troublemaker in the school. Unflinchingly he returned my gaze. Momentarily perturbed, I turned to the rest of the class and said 'Since you are here I advise you to do what I say or there will be trouble. Get changed quickly and go straight into the gymnasium.' Several boys exchanged exaggerated puzzled looks, shook their heads and began to undress slowly whilst others who sensed the menace in my voice hurriedly made their way into the gymnasium. As a kind of symbolic knock-out I used a count of ten to convince the others that I was serious. It is an understatement to say that the situation was tense. In fact, I felt that given time to collect themselves the story could be quite different. To minimize further disruption I taught a simple, arduous lesson which I directed, and to which the class responded. To lay down new rules was a bruising and exhausting exercise which took several weeks of painstaking and rigorous application. The hostility which my actions fostered died down gradually over the next few weeks for a number of reasons. The class became used to my domination and I, in turn, released my grip slightly—just enough to reduce the distance between us. Furthermore, rules can seldom be absolutely imposed. Quietness, for instance, is a matter of degree and opens up negotiations between teacher and taught. Furthermore, the nature of teaching physical education brings the teacher and children into close proximity to each other and the need to help the performer often required manual help from the teacher so that the reduction of physical isolation inherent in the direct dominative approach gives way to a closer relationship which is characteristic of the indirect helping approach. By the end of term our relationship had become friendly and co-operative within this background of control.'

Exercises

1. Compare and contrast the pupils' and teacher's definitions of the situation as described in this episode. List the factors which influence their definitions[2].
2. From your experience as a student-teacher and as a student identify
   (a) two instances when you have negotiated with children, and
   (b) two instances when you have negotiated with tutors.

To what extent was each outcome influenced by the authority structure?

3. From your knowledge of schools does it follow that a rigid imposition of authority brings about permanent changes in the behaviour of children? If your answer is positive, indicate the mechanisms which ensure this. If negative, what alternative strategies could be used which would be meaningful to children and ensure positive results?

4. Using the concepts, definition of the situation and bargaining for control[3] analyse the pattern of interaction of a formal gathering, for instance
   (a) a staff meeting
   (b) a student union meeting
   (c) an interdepartmental meeting
   (d) a sports club meeting

5. Projects 1 and 2 have adopted different sociological perspectives to describe teaching situations. These are currently known as the 'systems' and the 'action' perspectives. Outline the characteristics of each[4].

Notes and Bibliography

(1) HARGREAVES, D.H. (1972). "Interpersonal Relations and Education". London: Routledge and Kegan Paul. 228-266.

(2) COSIN, B.R., DALE, I.R., ESLAND, G.M. & SWIFT, D.F. (1971). "School and Society: A Sociological Reader". London: Routledge and Kegan Paul. 1-125.
     EGGLESTON, S.J. (1967). "The Social Context of the School". London: Routledge and Kegan Paul. 11-53.

(3) HARGREAVES, D.H. (1972). (see (1)). 93-227.
     THE SCHOOL AND SOCIETY COURSE TEAM. (1971). The construction of reality. In "School and Society, Units 1 and 2". Bletchley: The Open University Press.
     WALLER, W. (1967). "The Sociology of Teaching". London: Wiley. 292-318, 339-354.

(4) DAWE, A. (1971). The two sociologies. In K. Thompson & J. Tunstall (Eds.). "Sociological Perspectives". Harmondsworth: Penguin.
     EVETTS, J. (1973). "The Sociology of Educational Ideas". London: Routledge and Kegan Paul. 128-141.

Part 3　Analysis of
Documentary Evidence

Project 3

A SINGLE CASE SURVEY OF PHYSICAL EDUCATION IN A SCHOOL

Aims: 1. To analyse the results of a social survey of participation in extra-curricular physical activities in a single school.
2. To estimate the potential and limitations of survey findings for the planning of the curriculum of physical education.

Introduction

Social surveys or statistics produced by educational researchers, research foundations and government agencies provide an important set of data for the teacher who believes that curriculum planning will benefit from the careful consideration of research findings which were not assembled specifically with his or her school in mind. In fact, the amount of material potentially available for this purpose has increased considerably over the past two decades and some of the most imaginative and constructive curriculum designs may profit considerably from the careful analysis of this data.

A number of surveys which have concentrated upon the work of schools provide well documented and assiduously collated information on such diverse matters as curricular and extra-curricular participation in physical activities in grammar, secondary modern and technical schools; changes in sporting preferences of different age groups in relation to sex and social class; and the relationship between the objectives of teachers of physical education and the content of their programmes of activities[1]. Others have focused upon current preferences and participation rates of post-school adolescents and adults and have identified the circumstances in which people are most likely to continue to take an active part in physical recreation[2]. From a careful analysis and interpretation of this information, programmes of physical education can be formulated with some knowledge of the current interests of school and post-school groups.

Reanalysis, however, is likely to involve asking questions which the original study was not designed to answer and can lead to major difficulties of reinterpretation. For example, to learn that boys are more actively involved in sport than girls or that middle-class children participate in a wider range of activities than their working-class counterparts is only significant when these findings are weighed against the sex and social class mix of a particular school. Moreover, decisions about the curriculum will be based upon an informed consideration of other factors, some of which are open to sociological analysis, some to psychological, and in the end any judgement will be based upon hunches or informed guesswork. It should be realised, therefore, that surveys do not provide all that teachers will require to know to perform their jobs adequately. Nevertheless, careful consideration of these research findings will guide the selection of activities to be included in a physical education programme. Ultimately, it may well be the case that each school and each curriculum proposal should be investigated as a unique problem and that the origin of benefits to children and their future lives may differ from one situation to another.

Study Area and Procedure

This project utilizes data from a sample of 281 boys and 255 girls from the second year (13 year olds) and the fourth year (15 year olds) forms of a comprehensive school who participated in selected activities grouped into categories of indoor games, outdoor team games, outdoor pursuits and swimming[3]. Comparisons were made in terms of sex, age and social class. You are asked to study the table below and answer the questions which follow:

Social Class	Second Year (13 year olds)				Fourth Year (15 year olds)			
	I and II		IV and V		I and II		IV and V	
	Girls	Boys	Girls	Boys	Girls	Boys	Girls	Boys
Indoor	52.6	26.6	19.0	9.5	64.1	68.2	18.7	16.6
Outdoor Team	42.1	84.4	19.0	71.4	43.6	81.8	18.7	83.3
Outdoor Pursuits	57.9	42.2	19.0	57.1	46.2	72.7	25.0	50.0
Swimming	55.3	40.0	14.3	38.1	30.8	34.1	18.7	5.5
100%	38	45	21	21	39	44	16	18

Participation in selected activities in relation to social class of origin, excluding Class III, expressed as a percentage.

Exercises

1. Why do you think the investigator used social class, age and sex as his criteria of participation?
2. Compare the incidence of participation in each group of activities separately in terms of social class, age and sex. What conclusions do you draw?
3. From a review of relevant literature, give reasons for differences in participation[4].
4. Draw up the main hypotheses suggested by this data.
5. How useful is this information to the teacher of physical education?

Notes and Bibliography

(1) CENTRAL ADVISORY COUNCIL FOR EDUCATION. (1960). "15 to 18". London: H.M.S.O. Vol. II, 81-98, 166-174.

EMMETT, I. (1971). "Youth and Leisure in an Urban Sprawl". Manchester: University Press.

KANE, J. (1974). "Physical Education in Secondary Schools". London: Macmillan.

MORTON-WILLIAMS, R. & FINCH, S. (1968). "Schools Council Enquiry 1: Young School Leavers". London: H.M.S.O. 55-58, 169-190.

(2) The most comprehensive survey of sporting participation of young people and adults can be found in:

SILLITOE, K.K. (1969). "Planning for Leisure". London: H.M.S.O.

(3) CRUNDEN, C.C. (1970). Sport and social background: a study of 13 and 15 year old children. *Bull. of Phys. Educ.*, 8, 36-40.

(4) CHETWYND, H.R. (1960). "Comprehensive School—the Story of Woodberry Down". London: Routledge and Kegan Paul.

FORD, J. (1969). "Social Class and the Comprehensive School". London: Routledge and Kegan Paul.

KING, R. (1973). "School Organisation and Pupil Involvement: a Study of Secondary Schools". London: Routledge and Kegan Paul.

MILLER, T.W.G. (1961). "Values in the Comprehensive School". Edinburgh: Oliver and Boyd.

MONKS, T.G. (Ed.). (1970). "Comprehensive Education in Action". Slough: N.F.E.R.

ROSS, J.M., BUNTON, W.J., EVISON, P. & ROBERTSON, T.S. (1972). "A Critical Appraisal of Comprehensive Education". Slough: N.F.E.R.

SAUNDERS, E.D. & WITHERINGTON, K.S. (1970). Extra-curricular physical activities in secondary schools. *B.J. of Phys. Educ.*, 1, 10-14.

Project 4

A LARGE SCALE SURVEY OF SPORT AND LEISURE

Aims: 1. To analyse and compare the results of surveys of sport and leisure.
2. To examine and estimate the implications of survey research for the planning of the physical education programme.

Introduction

Sociology's contribution to the understanding of the effects of sport upon society in general and physical education in particular, has been distinctly limited. In fact, it is only recently that sociologists or physical educationists with sociological training have committed themselves to the study of the role of sport and physical education in society. This heightened interest has led to a great deal of theorizing about the role of sport in society, much of which has not been based upon the results of empirical research. On the other hand, research which has been conducted by sociologists has produced only fragments of knowledge upon which to build valid generalizations or theories about the social significance of sport and physical education[1]. In fact, the bulk of these studies has been devised for other purposes and the spin-off has been accidental rather than deliberate[2].

Despite this dismal record a number of investigations have furnished detailed information about the sporting characteristics of large representative samples of the population which are potentially valuable to teachers of physical education. However, problems similar to those outlined in the previous project arise in connection with the use of these research findings for curriculum planning. In particular, it is worthwhile noting that reinterpretation involves asking questions which the original studies were not constructed to answer.

Another problem with data collected by social survey techniques is that information as to causes is seldom explored. For example, a high correlation between sporting ability and scholastic achievement shows neither that sporting ability develops a greater desire to achieve academically, nor that academic success will produce a talented athlete. It merely indicates that there is a relationship, not that one is the cause of the other. Cause and association must not be confused.

A further drawback is encountered when we attempt to make valid generalizations from the results of more than one study as measures of behaviour are seldom standardized. Needless to say, each researcher devises his own measures of sporting behaviour according to the needs of his own study since each research project has its own unique measurement problems. Nevertheless, this does produce difficulties of interpretation.

Finally, survey material may not deal adequately with changes in sporting

39

participation. Tastes and preferences may be affected by a number of social pressures which change faster than they can be isolated for study. It cannot be assumed, for instance, that the present generation of school children will identify with and participate in physical activity currently in fashion with older age groups, even where school based programmes are formulated and taught skilfully and conscientiously. The capriciousness of social change will modify the effectiveness of a well planned programme of leisure-orientated physical activity in schools, even where plans have been based upon the results of empirical research.

However, the problem of the effect of change on patterns of sporting behaviour is not unique to the survey type of investigation.

Study and Procedure

To highlight some of the difficulties of interpretation you are asked to study the following tables (see APPENDIX 1A and 1B) which are abstracted from the nationwide study of 'Planning for Leisure'[3]. These tables list the games/sports in which men and women participated at least once per month, or more, for at least part of the preceding year in which the investigation took place. This provides useful material to compare with the results of your own observations and the participation pattern outlined in the previous project.

Exercises

1. One of the fundamental difficulties in analysing and comparing the results of sociological studies is that there is no common definition of terms. Failure to define terms may lead to misleading interpretation of data. To highlight this problem you are asked to define the terms: sport, games and recreation[4].
2. Compare and contrast the incidence of participation within and between age and sex groups and give reasons for differences.
3. Devise means of comparing this data with the data outlined in Project 3. Are there obvious discrepancies? What difficulties occurred in making these comparisons?
4. What are the main implications of this data for the programme of physical education in schools?
5. Compare and contrast the approaches adopted in Projects 1 and 2 with those adopted in Projects 3 and 4[5].

Notes and Bibliography

(1) The books listed below are key texts in the field of sociology of sport and games:
   AVEDON, E.M. & SUTTON-SMITH, B. (1971). "The Study of Games". London: Wiley
   CRATTY, B.J. (1967). "Social Dimensions of Physical Activity". New Jersey: Prentice-Hall.
   DUNNING, E. (Ed.). (1971) "The Sociology of Sport". London: Cass.
   LOY, J.W. & KENYON, G.S. (Eds.). (1969). "Sport, Culture and Society". London: Macmillan.
   LUSCHEN, G. (Ed.). (1970). "The Cross-Cultural Analysis of Sport and Games". Illinois: Stipes.

MANGAN, J.A. (Ed.). (1973). "Physical Education and Sport: Sociological and Cultural Perspectives". Oxford: Blackwell.

MCINTOSH, P.C. (1963). "Sport in Society". London: Watts.

SAGE, G.H. (Ed.). (1970). "Sport and American Society: Selected Readings". London: Addison-Wesley. In the related field of leisure, the following books provide additional insights into the role of sport and games in society:

ANDERSON, N. (1961). "Work and Leisure" London: Routledge and Kegan Paul.

DUMAZEDIER, J. (1967). "Toward a Society of Leisure". London: Collier-Macmillan.

JEPHCOTT, P. (1967). "Time of One's Own". Edinburgh: Oliver and Boyd.

LEIGH, J. (1971). "Young People and Leisure". London: Routledge and Kegan Paul.

PARKER, S.R. (1972). "The Future of Work and Leisure". London: Paladin.

ROBERTS, K. (1970). "Leisure". London: Longman.

SMIGEL, E.D. (Ed.). (1963). "Work and Leisure". New Haven: College and University Press.

SMITH, M.A., PARKER, S. & SMITH, C.S. (Eds.). (1973). "Leisure and Society in Britain". London: Lane.

(2) Case studies of urban and rural communities provide the most fruitful additional source of information. A review of these studies can be found in:

FRANKENBERG, R. (1966). "Communities in Britain". Harmondsworth: Penguin.

(3) SILLITOE, K.K. (1969). "Planning for Leisure". London: H.M.S.O. 237-238.

(4) See (1) above.

(5) In addition to the references cited in the previous projects the following texts will provide supplementary information:

MADGE, J. (1953). "The Tools of Social Science". London: Longmans.

MOSER, C.A. & KALTON, G. (1973). "Survey Methods in Social Investigation". London: Heinemann.

STACEY, M. (1969). "Methods of Social Research". London: Pergamon.

Appendix 1A

MALES

Games/sports in which took an active part regularly during the previous season	Persons who have completed full-time education aged —							ALL (including those in full-time education)
	15—18	19—22	23—26	27—30	31—45	46—60	61—70	
	%	%	%	%	%	%	%	%
Swimming (in pools)	44	29	26	27	21	5	2	17
Ballroom dancing	22	34	20	18	10	9	3	12
Soccer	41	26	26	14	8	1	—	10
Table tennis	30	16	14	14	8	3	1	9
Cricket	23	14	14	10	8	1	—	8
Fishing/angling	18	11	9	9	8	6	2	8
Ten-pin bowls	22	30	12	10	4	2	—	7
Golf	4	7	4	5	8	6	3	6
Bowls	3	3	3	3	5	6	9	6
Swimming (in sea)	9	16	7	10	6	4	1	6
Tennis	8	13	11	12	3	2	—	5
Fencing/archery/shooting	13	10	3	5	7	2	3	5
Badminton and squash	10	4	7	8	4	1	1	4
Athletics—gymnastics	14	5	5	3	—	—	—	3
Rowing and canoeing	8	9	6	1	2	1	—	3
Sailing	2	1	1	1	3	1	—	2
Boating	7	6	1	3	2	2	—	2
Rugby	6	7	4	1	1	—	—	2
Boxing/wrestling/judo	7	7	4	3	2	—	—	2
Pleasure-craft cruising	2	2	2	2	1	1	—	1
Motorised sports	3	1	4	2	1	1	—	1
Roller/ice skating	10	3	3	3	—	—	—	1
Horse riding	2	2	1	1	1	—	—	1
Any other activity	32	29	16	17	7	5	5	11

Appendix 1B

FEMALES

Games/sports in which took an active part regularly during the previous season	Persons who have completed full-time education aged —							ALL (including those in full time education)
	15—18	19—22	23—26	27—30	31—45	46—60	61—70	
	%	%	%	%	%	%	%	%
Ballroom dancing	49	35	20	16	6	7	3	12
Swimming (in pools)	31	17	17	10	9	3	—	8
Tennis	23	13	6	3	2	2	—	5
Table tennis	18	12	4	—	2	1	—	3
Ten-pin bowls	22	15	8	3	1	1	—	3
Swimming (in sea)	7	2	8	5	4	—	—	3
Badminton and squash	11	3	4	1	1	1	—	2
Golf	1	2	1	1	—	2	1	1
Rowing and canoeing	4	1	2	1	—	—	—	1
Boating	5	3	2	1	—	1	1	1
Fishing/angling	3	2	3	4	1	2	—	1
Horse riding	4	6	2	1	—	1	—	1
Roller/ice skating	12	6	3	1	—	—	—	1
Athletics/gymnastics	12	1	—	—	—	—	—	1
Bowls	1	1	—	—	—	1	1	1
Any other activity	39	22	9	7	8	9	2	10

Project 5

CONTENT ANALYSIS OF REPORTED SPORT AND PHYSICAL RECREATION

Aims: 1. To introduce techniques of content analysis of contemporary records of sport, physical recreation and physical education.
2. To identify and describe differences of coverage of sport and physical recreation and relate the findings to programmes of physical education in schools.

Introduction

One main thread running through sociological study is that there is an orderliness in society which the social scientist tries to discover[1]. Without some social order people would be unable to predict each other's behaviour and it would be impossible to interact or communicate in every day social situations. Based on the assumption that there is a social order which can be discovered, the sociologist has adopted modern research methods to identify social factors which govern every day life, subjected these to some form of test and from the analysis of the results of his investigations built up a body of knowledge which describes, even explains, aspects of order and disorder in society. Sport as part of our social order has come under this microscope. Emmett[2], for instance, identified factors such as age, sex, social class and school background as some of the important factors which influenced participation in physical activities amongst young people. She developed interview schedules which permitted deeper probing into the effects of these variables and provided a more precise and objective body of knowledge regarding sport and young people.

Not all sources of information arise in this way. Newspapers, radio, television, professional journals, periodicals and school magazines, for instance, present records and accounts of sport and physical education of a particular kind which are seldom subjected to close scrutiny or analysis. They provide sources of stimulus in everyday life which may influence, change or reaffirm preferences or opinions of some of the readers, viewers or listeners whilst failing to cater for others. Thus the field of mass communications can be used to study and identify the way in which ideas and values are presented to the public[3]. This project will examine the content of sport in newspapers.

Newspapers may present the same item of sport in diverse ways to cater for the needs and demands of different sporting audiences. Most provide coverage of sports that appeal to a mass audience, some extend their space to accommodate minority sports, and a few devote articles to contemporary issues such as international prestige and sport or sport and race.

In order to discover the underlying order of presentation of sports coverage it is necessary to code the content by the procedure known as content analysis[4]. First of all we must clarify what is desired from the materials, study the newspapers carefully, work out a set of rules to classify the content, then fit the classes to the content. Obviously sports sections can be analysed from a variety of points of view. By creating a quantitative index we can identify the proportion of coverage devoted to sport in relation to other news items or the proportion of space concerned with reporting or comments. On the other hand, a qualitative analysis will identify recurring themes presented in editorials or special articles and unearth the ideologies of those who present the 'facts' to us through the media of mass communication.

Study Area

This project will focus upon the quantitative analysis of the proportion of coverage given to sport within and between a number of newspapers to identify the following: the proportion of space each devotes in relation to all other *news* items (not advertisements); the proportion of space each sport occupies; and the types of sports reported. The purpose of the investigation is to ascertain whether some newspapers favour certain sports rather than others and whether any reasons for these differences can be inferred from the analysis of their contents.

Procedure

Two modes of analysis have been adopted in this project. The first requires the recording of the sports coverage over the period of one week (Monday to Saturday) of 'The Daily Telegraph', 'The Guardian', 'The Sun', and the 'Daily Express'. The second requires the analysis of content previously gathered from these newspapers (APPENDICES 1A and 1B)

Exercises

Mode One

1. Record the proportion of space each newspaper devotes to sport each day in relation to other *news* items (not advertisements).

Modes One and Two

2. Analyse the proportion of space each sport occupies and the types of sports covered. Compare and comment (APPENDIX 1A)
3. From the results of your analyses do you detect any biases? For instance, is there evidence to indicate that some newspapers reflect a 'class' or 'intellectual' bias? If so can you account for this?
4. Do you detect any particular differences in the *types* of content covered each day? If so, can this be accounted for? (APPENDIX 1B).
5. To what extent do the sports reported reflect programmes of physical education in

schools? For instance do 'quality' newspapers embody sports and games played at grammar schools and public schools?

6. Do all newspapers concentrate upon male rather than female sport? Give reasons for this bias if it occurs.

Notes and Bibliography

(1) COHEN, P.C. (1968). "Modern Social Theory". London: Heinemann. 18-33.

(2) EMMETT, I. (1967). "Youth and Leisure in an Urban Sprawl". Manchester: University Press.

(3) HOCH, P. (1974). "The Newspaper Game". London: Calder and Boyars.
KATZ, E. & LAZARSFELD, P.F. (1964). "Personal Influence". New York: The Free Press.
MCLUHAN, M.M. (1971). "Understanding Media: the extension of man". London: Sphere Books.
MCQUAIL, D. (1969). "Towards a Sociology of Mass Communications". London: Collier Macmillan.

(4) For accounts of the techniques of content analysis see
BERELSON, B. (1971). "Content Analysis in Communication Research". New York: Hafner.
SELLITZ, D., JAHODA, M., DEUTSCH, M. & COOK, S.W. (1966). "Research Methods in Social Research". London: Methuen. 330-342.

Appendix 1A

	Amount of space in inches			
	Express	Guardian	Sun	Telegraph
Cricket	421	408	694	270
Horse Racing	1750	857	1520	1037
Soccer	268	74	462	211
Archery	—	30	—	6½
Cycling	61	76	29¼	121
Dog Racing	115	—	26	—
Table Tennis	½	—	—	½
Motor Cycle Racing	69½	19	20	82
Boxing	52½	20	27	50
Rugby League	1	13½	2½	19½
Bowls	3	21½	19	57½
Golf	38¼	80	11¼	176
Athletics	81½	108½	46½	82
Speedway	11¾	—	16¾	3½
Tennis	79½	217	35¼	215
Croquet	—	15	—	½
Snooker	—	—	6	—
Motor Boat Racing	10	—	—	5
Sailing	2½	52	—	108
Show Jumping	2½	—	—	44
Motor Car Racing	45	12	—	42
Swimming	18	14½	—	6
Karate	—	6	—	—
Karting	—	12	—	—
Rugby Union	—	38½	—	51
Badminton	—	½	—	½
Squash	—	2½	—	3
Parachuting	—	12	—	40
Fencing	—	—	—	2
Rowing	—	—	—	25½
Wrestling	—	—	—	3
Water Skiing	—	—	—	½
Angling	—	—	58	—
Articles	235	76	86	—
Total Sports Coverage	3265½	2165½	3059½	2662½
Total Other News	9065	15796	5964	13440

Appendix 1B

	Express						Guardian						Sun						Telegraph					
	M	T	W	T	F	S	M	T	W	T	F	S	M	T	W	T	F	S	M	T	W	T	F	S
Cricket	53	80	18	61	92	117	91	60	32	65	84	76	119	77	86	104	209	100	84	84	38	123	120	12
Horse Racing	216	213	416	384	190	331	159	110	192	120	122	154	240	153	449	246	156	276	160	168	172	201	160	176
Soccer	30	18	68	90	28	34	10	11	6½	20	5½	21	80	85	90	113	20	65	48	34	31	59	24	15
Archery	—	—	—	—	—	—	—	30	—	—	—	—	—	—	—	—	—	—	—	—	—	—	6	½
Cycling	18½	16	6	4½	7	9	20	15	1	16	15	9	9	5	—	4¼	5	6	42	14	4	20	19	22
Dog Racing	7	24	19	20	12	30	—	—	—	—	—	—	4	—	7	7	1	7	—	—	—	—	—	—
Table Tennis	½	—	—	—	—	—	—	—	—	—	—	—	—	—	—	—	—	—	½	—	—	—	—	—
Motor Cycle Racing	3½	20	10	—	15	21	—	13	—	—	—	6	—	14	—	2	—	4	11	26	10	7	20	8
Boxing	—	8½	42	—	—	2	—	—	20	—	—	—	—	20	—	7	—	—	—	13	35	—	2	—
Rugby League	1	—	—	—	—	—	12	—	—	1½	—	—	—	2	—	—	—	½	13	2½	—	4	—	—
Bowls	—	—	2	—	1	—	—	4	4½	4	4	5	5	4	3	5	1	1	—	14	12	9	10½	12
Golf	½	1	½	¼	11	25	22	3½	1½	21	17	15	4	1¼	—	4	1	1	14	12	15	39	53	43
Athletics	50	—	9½	—	2	20	66	7	17	1½	15	2	31	—	15	—	—	½	44	—	21	6	—	11
Speedway	—	10½	½	½	—	¼	—	—	—	—	—	—	6	—	—	¼	10	½	—	—	—	½	3	—
Tennis	8	9½	20	2	9	31	—	40	54	46	29	48	14	6	6	6¼	1	2	27	39	33	40	34	42
Croquet	—	—	—	—	—	—	15	—	—	—	—	—	—	—	—	—	—	—	—	—	—	—	½	—
Snooker	—	—	—	—	—	—	—	—	—	—	—	—	—	—	—	—	6	—	—	—	—	—	—	—
Motor Boat Racing	—	—	—	—	—	10	—	—	—	—	—	—	—	—	—	—	—	—	—	—	—	—	5	—
Sailing	½	—	—	—	—	2	7	13	—	14	12	6	—	—	—	—	—	—	24	19	18	15	16	16
Show Jumping	2	—	—	—	—	½	—	—	—	—	—	—	—	—	—	—	—	—	11	—	5	10	12	6
Motor Car Racing	13	—	5	—	27	—	12	—	—	—	—	—	—	—	—	—	—	—	18	—	—	—	15	9
Swimming	—	—	18	—	—	—	13	—	—	—	1	½	—	—	—	—	—	—	6	—	—	—	—	—
Karate	—	—	—	—	—	—	6	—	—	—	—	—	—	—	—	—	—	—	—	—	—	—	—	—
Karting	—	—	—	—	—	—	12	—	—	—	—	—	—	—	—	—	—	—	—	—	—	—	—	—
Rugby Union	—	—	—	—	—	—	33	—	5½	—	—	—	—	—	—	—	—	—	28	22	1	—	—	—
Badminton	—	—	—	—	—	—	—	—	¼	—	¼	—	—	—	—	—	—	—	—	—	—	—	½	—
Squash	—	—	—	—	—	—	½	—	—	—	2	—	—	—	—	—	—	—	—	—	—	—	3	—
Parachuting	—	—	—	—	—	—	—	—	12	—	—	—	—	—	—	—	—	—	40	—	—	—	—	—
Fencing	—	—	—	—	—	—	—	—	—	—	—	—	—	—	—	—	—	—	2	—	—	—	—	—
Rowing	—	—	—	—	—	—	—	—	—	—	—	—	—	—	—	—	—	—	—	—	6½	8	11	—
Wrestling	—	—	—	—	—	—	—	—	—	—	—	—	—	—	—	—	—	—	—	3	—	—	—	—
Water Skiing	—	—	—	—	—	—	—	—	—	—	—	—	—	—	—	—	—	—	—	—	—	½	—	—
Angling	—	—	—	—	—	—	—	—	—	—	—	—	—	24	—	—	32	2	—	—	—	—	—	—

Part 4 Observation and
Analysis of Group
Behaviour

Project 6

OBSERVATION OF NORMS OF BEHAVIOUR IN A PHYSICAL EDUCATION
CONTEXT

Aims: 1. To make a systematic observation of the recreational use of physical
education facilities.
2. To discover ways of representing the collected data and to consider the
possible implications of the observed norms for programmes of physical
education and physical recreation.

Introduction

Among the most important of the sociologist's functions is the observation and
recording of the behaviour of human groups. Explanations as well as predictions and
straightforward statements about the behaviour of human groups can be based upon
the empirical data of controlled observation. In the main, the sociologist is stimulated
by motives which emanate from his own desire to know more about his subject and the
information adds, not only to his knowledge, but to the general body of knowledge
that is, or supports, sociological theory. Less frequently information collected by the
sociologist is taken and used by other agencies for their own purposes.

The usefulness and reliability of any information depends upon the accuracy with
which it is observed and recorded. An essential preliminary stage, therefore, includes a
statement of the limits of the observations, a clear definition of all terms and categories
to be used and an agreement upon a standard form of procedure. This inevitably puts
limitations upon the data and restricts its application. Others using or reading the data
must be aware of its limitations and must be able to avoid the common error of
generalization from data collected in specific situations. At the same time, it will be
seen that the clear definitions and adherence to a standard procedure confer a high
degree of accuracy and reliability on the data within its limits.

Study Area

In the planning of new facilities for physical education and in the timetabling of
existing facilities, alongside other factors, it is important to take account of demand.
While this may be of minor importance when school use is considered, because of the
largely compulsory programme and possibly limited number of activities, it must be
given a higher priority in determining recreational provision or allocation. Experience
has shown, for instance that it is uneconomical in every way to provide a large fully
equipped gymnasium which cannot be adapted to alternative uses. In practice, it is wise
to estimate both school and non-school requirements so that adequate provision is

made for both educational and recreational activities. In particular, recreational groups will be acutely aware that facilities planned to meet the needs of traditional physical education programmes will be inappropriate for their purposes. Conversely, recent thinking in physical education has called into question the adequacy of existing facilities and multi-purpose halls/gymnasia are now strongly advocated to cater for a wide range of physical activities. The prevention of difficulties such as those described lies in careful planning based upon accurate assessment of requirements.

The popularity of an activity gauged by the number of participants is an easy parameter to assess, and where special equipment or space is required this is very important for reasons of economy. A complementary parameter is the popularity of a particular facility irrespective of the purpose for which it is used since to some extent this will reflect the flexibility and adaptability of the facility. This becomes more important when limited provision and multi-purpose use are envisaged.

The provision of supervision and instruction is an allied area to those already discussed. Levels here are frequently arbitrary and only minimally dependent upon considerations of safety and preferred group size.

Procedure

1. Students are asked to observe and record the use made of a selection of the facilities in the following list. The facilities may be those on campus or in the local community provided that the limitations of either choice are noted when drawing up norms and implications.

   Gymnasium (since this is the most commonly provided facility more than one may be included in the survey)
   Sports Hall
   Swimming Pool
   Outdoor, all-weather area
   School (or church) Hall
   Specialist rooms, for example, weight training, table tennis, judo

   The survey should include observations made nightly (or twice nightly) for the period of one or two weeks. Records should be made of the date and time; the facility, its size and equipment, total number present, activity(ies) in progress; size of working sub-groups, for example, the number of people working alone, in pairs, in threes, or in larger sized groups; and such other details as it is relevant and possible to collect.

2. Where possible (and this is clearly easier with on campus facilities or in a purpose-built sports and recreation complex) observe and record participation levels by activity. Choose a range of activities which includes examples of single sex and mixed; individual, pair and group (or team); competitive and non-competitive sports or pursuits.

   It may be desirable to agree on the categories to be used and to define these through discussion.

Exercises

1. Present the information you have collected under separate category headings by means of the most appropriate bar diagrams, pie charts or frequency polygons[1].
2. Present the information in a composite form by means of a single table with clearly headed columns, totals and means.
3. From the recorded observations determine which facility is most intensively used and consider how this could be explained. Similarly determine which facility is least intensively used, and consider the reasons which might account for this.
4. Referring to these observations consider which activities appear to be most popular according to the numbers participating and which types of activity appear to be the most preferred.
5. In the light of the observations made what modifications to the existing facilities would make them more appropriate to the requirements of the population they serve?
6. Prepare a statement describing the type of facilities for physical recreation that would be most suitable for a community similar to the one for which your data has been recorded[2].

Notes and Bibliography

(1) CONNOLLY, T.G. & SLUCKIN, W. (1962). "Statistics for the Social Sciences'. London: Cleaver-Hume Press. 1-17.
LOVEDAY, R. (1971). "A First Course in Statistics". Cambridge: University Press. 94-111.
MORONEY, M.J. (1951). "Facts from Figures". Harmondsworth: Penguin. 19-33.
(2) BIRCH, J.G. (1971). "Indoor Sports Centres". Sports Council Studies 1. London: H.M.S.O.
FRANKENBERG, R. (1966). "Communities in Britain". Harmondsworth: Penguin.
KLEIN, J. (1965). "Samples from English Cultures". Vol. 1. London: Routledge and Kegan Paul.
LEIGH, J. (1971). "Young People and Leisure". London: Routledge and Kegan Paul.
PARKER, S.R. (1972). "The Future of Work and Leisure". London: Paladin.
ROBERTS, K. (1970). "Leisure". London: Longman.
SMITH, M.A., PARKER, S. & SMITH, C.S. (Eds.). (1973). "Leisure and Society in Britain". London: Lane.

Project 7

SOCIOMETRIC ANALYSIS OF SMALL GROUPS IN PHYSICAL EDUCATION

Aims:
1. To introduce the sociomatrix and sociogram as steps towards the interpretation and understanding of sociometric data.
2. To explore the usefulness of the sociometric choice test as a means of investigating the structure of small groups in physical education classes.

Introduction

'The mathematical study of psychological properties of population, the experimental technique of and the results obtained by the application of quantitative and qualitative methods is called sociometry'.[1]

It is a science which has developed techniques for discovering the structure of groups from the expressed preferences of group members for companions or associates in any given work or play situation. It was the intention of Moreno, the founder of the sociometric movement, that preferences expressed by group members would be used as the basis for the re-organization of the group. There is reported evidence that sociometrically determined groups in factories proved more efficient and that sociometrically determined groups in schools and other institutions were more satisfactory than groups which were randomly selected. Recently, developments in sociology and social-psychology have led to an increased use of sociometric techniques purely as research tools. The most frequently used device is the sociometric choice test. In physical education contexts this kind of test has been administered with relative ease to games teams, camping groups, school forms and year groups. The criterion of a sociometric choice test will have been carefully worded by the investigator to indicate clearly to the subjects the population from whom the choices are to be made, as well as the number and purpose of the choices: for example, write down the names of the THREE boys in this form with whom you would like to work in the gymnasium lessons. The number of choices permitted depends upon the situation under investigation and can be varied as can the purpose of choice, in this very adaptable measure. It is usual to allow respondents the opportunity to express strong feelings against potential associates by including a rejection clause such as 'If there are any boys with whom you would definitely *not* like to work in the gymnasium write their names here .... ' (An example of a simple sociometric test can be found in APPENDIX I.)

The results of sociometric choice tests may be analysed in two main ways:

by means of a choice matrix, or

in the form of a sociogram.

The choice matrix consists of a matrix with as many rows and columns as there are members in the group under investigation. The columns and rows are accorded the name of one of the subjects and then each subject's choices and rejections are plotted in turn in the columns of those receiving his choice. At the end of this process the individual's acceptance score may be derived by subtracting the number of rejections from the number of choices in his column: acceptance score (sociometric status for the criterion of the test) equals total choices minus total rejections.

Evans[2] describes a method of re-arranging the rows and columns of the choice matrix in such a way 'as to make the structure of the group apparent.' From the resultant sociomatrix the completion of a sociogram is a relatively easy step and the use of Northway's[3] target method produces a clear representation of the sub-groups structure. An alternative method to that of Evans which can be completed directly from the sociometric choice test, thus eliminating the stage requiring matrix manipulation, defines the principles to be observed in allocating individuals to groups. Although there remains some element of trial and error the principles cover most eventualities and where placement is not immediately clear, reference should be made to the levels of choice expressed so that a person is grouped, as far as possible, with the person of his first choice. The principles are as follows:

1. Obvious sub-groups revealed by the sociomatrix should be adhered to.
2. Isolates should be placed in the group containing the boy of their first choice. The next highest choice should be observed if rejections do not permit placement with the first choice.
3. Boys expressing reciprocal choices should be placed in the same group.
4. A boy receiving a large number of choices may be removed from his natural group to allow the inclusion of an isolate. The boy removed from his group in this way should be placed with a boy who chooses him.
5. Rejections must always be respected.

The choice matrix provides the group members' acceptance scores and thus an indication of the range of sociometric status which can be related to other parameters in a investigation with interesting results. For this reason many researches only take the results of a sociometric test as far as the choice matrix and neglect the sociogram completely. A more balanced view regards the sociomatrix and the sociogram as complementary methods of representing the same data.

Study Area

In physical education reference is made continually to the need for grouping. Consideration is given in teacher education to the possible advantages and disadvantages of grouping for games or swimming according to ability while the practising and experienced teacher recognizes the importance of size and maturation as factors which need to be taken into account when pairing or grouping for physical contests and contact games. In other aspects of education, mixed ability groups are currently creating a fashion which has long been the accepted norm in physical education.

Mixed ability groups may be not only acceptable but desirable in certain physical education situations. Whereas randomly determined groups may appear to ensure fairness and avoid favouritism, and groups equated for height provide an evenness at some stages in volleyball and basketball, there is some evidence that positive advantages may accrue to the members of sociometrically determined groups engaged in other minor team games[4]. It may also be advantageous to use sociometrically determined groups for expeditions and camping where the ability to work together effectively and live together amicably for a period of time is important for safety as well as enjoyment.

There is some evidence also that friendship choice, which can be discovered efficiently and reliably by means of a sociometric test, determines to some extent the patterns of passing in games situations. Klein & Christiansen[5] showed that passing followed the friendship patterns in basketball teams playing against opposition of moderate standard.

In numerous other studies[6] attempts have been made to explain status in terms of a variety of physical abilities and skills. The discovery of a strong or causal association would be an important step for the physical educationist and the sociologist; for both it would lead to a more complete knowledge of the behaviour of groups.

Procedure

Students are asked to construct a sociometric choice test which could be administered to a school form or student team to discover whether there is a relationship between sociometric (friendship) status and skill or knowledge in the criterion situation. When the test has been constructed it should be administered with proper introduction and care over procedure to an appropriate group of between 10 and 30 subjects (see Appendix 1).

Exercises

1. From the completed sociometric test papers construct
   (a) a choice matrix for both criteria
   (b) a sociomatrix on the friendship criterion
   (c) a sociogram (see APPENDIX II) on the friendship criterion.
2. From the choice matrices derive acceptance scores on friendship and skill (or knowledge). Identify the stars, isolates, rejectees (see APPENDIX III) etc. in each and graph the distributions. Note any particular features of the distribution curves. Calculate the rank order correlation between the two sets of data[7]. What do you deduce from the result?
3. Examine the sociogram and the sociomatrix to identify sub-groups and consider the indications of cohesiveness and cleavage within the group.
4. What further educational implications might be drawn from the results?

Notes and Bibliography

(1) MORENO, J.L. (1933). "Psychological Organisation of Groups in the Community". Year Book of Mental Deficiency. Boston: 1.

(2) EVANS, K.M. (1962). "Sociometry and Education". London: Routledge and Kegan Paul. 24-28.

(3) (a) NORTHWAY, M.L. (1951). A Note on the Use of Target Sociograms. *Sociometry*, 14, 235-236.
   (b) NORTHWAY, M.L. (1959). "A Primer of Sociometry". Toronto: University Press. 22-25.

(4) WHITE, G.B. (1966). A Sociometric Investigation of the Effects of Three Different Types of Indoor Lesson in Physical Education. *Research Papers in Physical Education*, 2, 47-53.

(5) KLEIN, M. & CHRISTIANSEN, G. (1969). Group Composition, Group Structure and Group Effectiveness of Basketball Teams, In J.W. Loy & G.S. Kenyon. (Eds.). Sport, Culture and Society. New York: McMillan. 397-408.

(6) The following are examples of texts which identify status differences:
   COLEMAN, J.S. (1961). "The Adolescent Society". London: Free Press of Glencoe.
   CRATTY, B.J. (1967). "Social Dimensions of Physical Activity". New Jersey: Prentice Hall.
   HARGREAVES, D.H. (1967)."Social Relations in a Secondary School". London: Routledge and Kegan Paul.
   KING, R. (1969). "Values and Involvement in a Grammar School". London: Routledge and Kegan Paul.
   LAMBERT, L. & MILLHAM, S. (1974). "The Hothouse Society". Harmondsworth: Pelican.
   MANGAN, J.A. (1973). Some sociological concomitants of Secondary School Physical Education. In J.A. Mangan (Ed.). "Physical Education and Sport: Sociological and Cultural Perspectives". Oxford: Blackwell. 23-24.
   START, K.B. (1967). Substitution of games performance as a means of achieving status amongst secondary school boys. *B.J. Sociol.*, 17, 300-305.

(7) CONNOLLY, T.G. & SLUCKIN, W. (1962). "Statistics for the Social Sciences". London: Cleaver-Hume Press.

Appendix I

Confidential

THE SOCIOMETRIC CHOICE TEST

Write your own name here . . . .

In the spaces below write the names of the *THREE* boys in this form whom you choose as your friends.

1. . . . .

2. . . . .

3. . . . .

If there are any boys with whom you could not possibly be friends, write their names here.

. . . .

. . . .

In the spaces below write the names of the *THREE* boys in this form whom you would choose to go with you on a camping expedition.

1. . . . .

2. ....

3. ....

If there are any boys with whom you could not possibly go on a camping expedition, write their names here.

....

....

Appendix II Northway's Target Sociogram

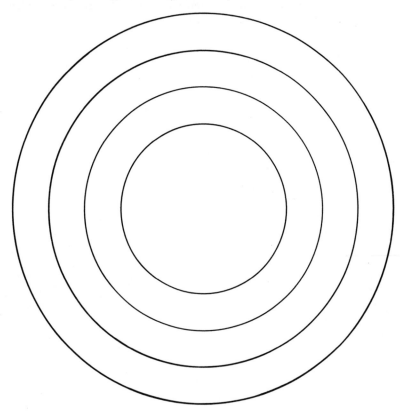

Appendix III A Glossary of Relevant Sociometric Terms

Star   —   an individual for whom many choices are expressed; one who is overchosen.

Isolate   —   one who has none of his choices reciprocated. The term is sometimes applied to an individual who receives no choices i.e. has a zero acceptance score.

Rejectee — one who is unchosen and also rejected by others in the group i.e. has a negative acceptance score.

Mutual — an individual who is paired with another by the exchange or reciprocation of choices.

Dyad — (also referred to as a mutual pair) two individuals who express choices for one another.

Triangle — three persons expressing choices for one another.

Leader — a person who, by virtue of his high acceptance score, is judged to be the central figure in a group.

Outsider/Fringer — one who has few choice connections with the group; an isolate or individual who has a low acceptance score.

Project 8

INTERACTION RECORDING OF BEHAVIOUR IN GAMES SITUATIONS

Aims: 1. To introduce interaction recording and to give some experience in its practical application.
2. To highlight some of the social processes which occur during games playing and to analyse their implications for teaching and learning.

Introduction

Interaction occurs between persons and between members of groups and teams. It can be regarded as a communication network indicating the channels along which verbal exchanges pass between members and may be extended to include other non-verbal or symbolic exchanges which include gestures and facial expressions seen to be indicative of feelings and attitudes[1]. In the context of physical activity, especially in games, symbolic interaction includes the patterns and frequency of passing between team-mates[2] and in a somewhat different view, the patterns of passing of all players round a moving ball[3]. It is an important component of group processes since group norms are developed and communicated through interaction.

Study Area and Procedure

1. Students are required to observe a basketball game and record,
   (a) the verbal interaction,
   (b) the symbolic interaction,
   which takes place. Two forms of interaction recording sheet are shown in the APPENDIX: Ia for verbal interaction; Ib for symbolic interaction.
   Note: It is recommended that observers work in pairs, one watching the game and commentating e.g. player four to five, player five to ten, player ten to six etc., and the other recording this information on the recording sheet.
   It is advisable to check the official score sheet prior to the commencement of the game to ensure that the names and numbers are correctly entered on the recording sheet.
   If possible, a record should be kept of the length of time each player spends on court.

2. At half time in the game under observation the recorders are asked to consult and place the players in each team in rank order on the criterion of basketball ability.
3. At the end of the game recorders should consult the official score sheet in order to extract the following information required for the exercises.

(a) individual scores

(b) individual personal fouls committed

(c) the name and number of the official captain of each team

(d) the name of the official coach of each team

(e) the team scores at half time and full time.

4. From the interaction recording sheets calculate the total verbal interaction each player (i) initiated and (ii) received, and the total symbolic interaction each player (i) initiated and (ii) received.

Exercises

1. (a) Which player initiated most verbal interaction?

   (b) Which player initiated most symbolic interaction?

   (c) Which had most verbal interaction directed to him?

   (d) Which player was the subject of most symbolic interaction?

2. Are the holders of extreme high and low positions in the above, i.e. 1(a), (b), (c) and (d) also identifiable as holding high or low positions on other criteria for which data has been collected?

   (Inspection may reveal this at this stage).

3. Where relationships appear to exist by the inspection method of 2 above, express the relationship as a hypothesis and test it by applying Spearman's Rank Order Correlation technique to the relevant data[4].

4. Is there a relationship between the position which a player occupies on the court and his level of verbal and/or symbolic interaction?

5. What other relationships are observable or could be postulated as a result of this observation?

6. Of what group processes has this project made you aware and what is their importance

   (a) in physical activity?

   (b) to the physical educator?

Notes and Bibliography

(1) ARGYLE, M. (1973). "Social Encounters". Harmondsworth: Penguin. 9.

GOFFMAN, E. (1961). "Encounters". New York: Bobbs-Merrill. 34-66.

MAULDON, E. (1973). Communication through movement. In J.D. Brooke and H.A. Whiting. (Eds.). "Human Movement—A Field of Study". London: Kimpton. 97-107.

GRUSKY, O. (1969). The Effects of Formal Structure on Managerial Recruitment: a Study of Baseball Organisation. In J.W. Loy and G.S. Kenyon. (Eds.). "Sport, Culture and Society". New York: McMillan.

(2) KLEIN, M. & CHRISTIANSEN, G. (1969). Group Composition Group Structure and Group Effectiveness of Basketball Teams. In J.W. Loy & G.S. Kenyon. (Eds.). "Sport, Culture and Society". New York: McMillan.

(3) ELIAS, N. & DUNNING, E. (1963). Dynamics of Group Sports with Special Reference to Football. *B.J. Sociol.*, 14, 388-402.

(4) CONNOLLY, T.G. & SLUCKIN, W. (1962). "Statistics for the Social Sciences". London: Cleaver-Hume Press. 150-151.

Appendix 1A Interaction Recording Matrix Verbal

							Total Initiated
Total Received							

Enter the names and/or numbers of the players in the left hand column and, in the same order, in the top row of the matrix.
When a player speaks to another player put a tick or tally in the column of the player he speaks to.
If a player speaks, but to none in particular, write an "S" in his row but in an unused box.
Use the bottom row and the last column to total the speech initiated and received.

Appendix 1B Interaction Recording Matrix Symbolic (Passing)

								Total Initiated
Total Received								

Enter the names and/or numbers of the players in the left hand column and, in the same order, in the top row of the matrix.
When a player passes to another put a tick or tally in the column of the player he passes to.
Use the bottom row and the last column to total the passes given and received.

Part 5　Questionnaire Design

Project 9

EXPLORATORY, SEMI-STRUCTURED INTERVIEWS OF TEACHERS OF PHYSICAL EDUCATION

Aims: 1. To introduce means of collecting data by personal interview
2. To examine the relationship between hypothesis testing and theory building in physical education.

Introduction

Interviews can be conducted in a variety of ways, structured, semi-structured and unstructured. The advantage of structured over unstructured interviews is that questions are formulated in advance and the range of responses is pre-determined so that the interviewer is not dependent upon his own judgement to decide which questions to ask and the interviewee is only permitted a limited number of responses. On the other hand, the unstructured interview allows the interviewee to dictate the course of the interview with some direction or orientation from the interviewer and this is a useful device in pilot studies or exploratory investigations.

Between these two extremes lies the semi-structured interview where all decisions concerning what to look for are constructed in a schedule of questions which are left open-ended to permit variable responses from the interviewee. This technique produces a richness of information which is not uncovered by the limited response type question. For instance, in answer to the question 'are you in complete charge of physical education in the school?—Yes/No (delete which is *not* applicable)' the responses are very limited. The question does not uncover situations where part of the programme of activities is controlled by other members of the staff of the school. Nevertheless, the semi-structured interview produces problems of interpretation especially where more than one interviewer is being used. Anyone familiar with interviewing of this type is aware of the difficulties of codifying a variety of responses to facilitate an accurate comparison of results.

It can be argued, however, that unstructured exploratory types of enquiry are more suited to the study of physical education where few significant sociological studies have been carried out which give clear guidelines for research. Unstructured enquiries which are sometimes a great deal more structured than is admitted demand great skill from the interviewer, produce problems of codifying the results and perhaps most important of all are guided by a number of hidden or implicit assumptions or values which influence the observation and selection of particular patterns of behaviour. This is not unique to sociological enquiry, for in everyday life observations are made which are based upon a number of untested assumptions about human nature.

This problem can be partially overcome by the development of hypotheses which can be generated from a review of the literature of the problem area in general, as a 'hunch', or as an educated guess. Where the hypothesis is related to a body of theory contained in the research literature, the results may lead to the modification or elaboration of that theory and provide a more substantive body of knowledge about the sociology of physical education[1].

Hypothesis directed enquiry provides guidelines for the development of a series of questions which can be incorporated into a semi-structured interview situation. The interviewer has the schedule before him for completion during or after the interview, but the open-ended nature of the questions allows him freedom to decide how best to secure the information. However, the problem of recording and codifying this information should not be underestimated. The project which follows illustrates the usefulness of hypothesis directed enquiry.

Study Area

One problem area which has interested physical educationists over the years is the effect of tradition upon patterns of physical activity in schools. A review of literature will show that tradition, which is defined as loyalty to long established ways of doing things, is a powerful constraint upon a teacher's ability to change the programme of physical activities of the school.[2]. The older the school the more likelihood that cultural tradition will restrict the freedom of the physical education department to effect change. Consequently, secondary modern schools will be less restricted by tradition than grammar schools which were built pre-war. Research in this area leads to the development of the following proposition:

> The physical education department is likely to have less autonomy in a school where the policy relating to physical education is affected by traditional elements, and that this is more likely to occur in grammar than in secondary modern schools.

Statement of Hypotheses

Further reading would indicate that three inter-related hypotheses are inherent in this proposition.
1. That schools bound down by tradition will reflect an unchanging physical education programme.
2. That the stronger the tradition of the school, the less autonomy the physical education department will have for change.
3. That where physical activities are not part of the established tradition of the school, change is more likely to occur.

Procedure

Questionnaire design (see Appendix for Questionnaire)[3]
The initial difficulty in drafting a questionnaire is to determine the number of

questions which will explore each hypothesis thoroughly. In an exploratory study, this may be decided arbitrarily on the result of reading or in consultation with other professional colleagues. However, to prevent ambiguities of response or difficulties of interpretation copies of the draft questionnaire should be circulated amongst the members of staff or other competent persons for comment. Some hypotheses may require the analysis of documents, such as school records, to gain accurate information, whilst the validation of others will require only one question. Perhaps the most important factor of all is the time element required to conduct the interview. Some may last for over one hour but normally twenty to thirty minutes is recommended. The order in which the questions are posed is another problem. This can be solved by conducting the interview in the way you would normally conduct an informal conversation. The order of the questions can be re-established later when the results are being analysed.

Questionnaire Administration

In this project you are asked to interview two members of staff, one of whom has taught in a long established grammar school, the other in a secondary modern school. Two methods can be used to collect the information. Notes may be taken on a schedule already prepared. Alternatively, a tape recorder may be used.

In order to gain the full co-operation of teachers it will be necessary to assure them that the results of the study will be carefully safeguarded so that they will remain anonymous in any subsequent publication. When they are convinced of the value of the study few objections will be raised.

Further Considerations

In this study, it is unrealistic to assume that the physical education department controls all curricular and extra-curricular physical activities, compulsory or non-compulsory. The frame of reference for physical education should be explained to the interviewees as 'all the activities which are planned and guided by the physical education department which are carried out individually or in a group, inside or outside the school during the time set aside on the timetable for compulsory physical education.'

Analysis and Interpretation of Data

Since this study is guided by hypotheses which are exploratory, the findings can only be tentatively assessed. However, it should be possible to analyse the content of the answers to abstract the common factors associated with the hypotheses. This could lead to a more objective definition of the differences which reflect the tradition/non-tradition dichotomy. At a later stage, this evidence could be translated into a pilot study which would provide the basis of more objective analyses.

Exercises

1. Record the responses of the teachers to the questions.

2. Analyse the content of the responses in relation to the stated hypotheses.
3. Describe the implications of the findings for the planning of the curriculum in different types of schools.
4. Re-write the questionnaire in the light of the results of the investigation.

Notes and Bibliography

(1) BURROUGHS, G.E.R. (1971). "Design and Analysis in Educational Research". Birmingham: University of Birmingham Monograph No. 8. 16-21, 99-104.
(2) The following texts offer useful insights into the functions of tradition in comprehensive, grammar, public and secondary modern schools:
FORD, J. (1969). "Social Class and the Comprehensive School". London: Routledge and Kegan Paul.
HARGREAVES, D.H. (1967). "Social Relations in a Secondary School". London: Routledge and Kegan Paul.
JACKSON, B. & MARSDEN, D. (1961). "Education and the Working Class". London: Routledge and Kegan Paul.
KING, R. (1969). "Values and Involvement in a Grammar School". London: Routledge and Kegan Paul.
KING, R. (1973). "School Organisation and Pupil Involvement: A Study of Secondary Schools". London: Routledge and Kegan Paul.
LACEY, C. (1970). "Hightown Grammar: the School as a Social System". Manchester: University Press.
LAMBERT, R. (1968). "The Hothouse Society". London: Weidenfeld and Nicolson.
MILLER, T.W.G. (1961). "Values in the Comprehensive School". Edinburgh: Oliver and Boyd.
PARTRIDGE, J. (1966). "Life in a Secondary Modern School". Harmondsworth: Penguin.
SAUNDERS, E.D. & WITHERINGTON, K.S. (1970). "Extra-curricular Physical Activities in Secondary Schools". *B.J. Phys. Educ.*, 1, 10-14.
SAUNDERS, E.D. (1971). "Aspects of Change and Physical Education in the Social System of the School". *Scottish Bull. of Phys. Educ.*, 8.
STEVENS, F. (1961). "The Living Tradition". London: Hutchinson.
TAYLOR, W. (1963). "The Secondary Modern School". London: Faber.
WAKEFORD, J. (1969). "The Cloistered Elite". London: Macmillan.
WILKINSON, R.H. (1964). "The Prefects, British Leadership and the Public School Tradition". Oxford: University Press.
(3) BURROUGHS, G.E.R. (1971). (see 1) above. 22-51.

Appendix

Questions Relating to Hypothesis I

Questions Administered to Heads of Physical Education Departments.

Question 1 To what extent has the physical education programme changed over the past five years?*
Question 2 With regard to the appointment of specialist and non-specialist staff who might be expected to assist with the normal curriculum physical education programme, to what extent does the particular sporting speciality of an applicant influence his appointment?
Question 3 To what extent is the programme of physical education determined by the specific expertise of both specialist and non-specialist members of staff?

*Note that accurate answers to this question would be more fruitfully explored through the analyses of school records, magazines, reports etc. In fact, if the study was being carried out amongst existing schools, this evidence would be gathered in this way providing documentary evidence was available.

Questions Relating to Hypothesis II

Question 1 Are you in complete charge of physical education within the school?

Question 2 Have you complete freedom to determine the physical education programme?

Question 3 Do other members of staff who are not in the department assist with curriculum physical education and, if so, how much control do you have over what and how they teach?

Question 4 Do members of the physical education department or members of staff who assist with curriculum physical education attend physical education courses? If so, which courses?

Question 5 Would it be possible for you to introduce a new physical activity into the programme or discontinue one already part of the programme?

Question 6 Does the Head expect to be involved in policy decisions relating to physical·education and where you have effected a change has it been necessary to obtain his support?

Question 7 To what extent does the Head or staff express the desire for changes in the physical education programme?

Questions Relating to Hypothesis III

Question 1 Regardless of whether or not you consider it desirable, would it be possible to introduce modern educational dance into your programme?

Question 2 Do you have an understanding within the department regarding which activities should be covered during physical education lessons? Is each teacher given freedom to teach what and how he wants to teach?

Question 3 Have any of the activities you have introduced interfered with or replaced established parts of the programme?

Question 4 Have you or members of your department been responsible for introducing inter-school competition in physical activities that were not part of the programme when you were appointed?

Project 10

STRUCTURED INTERVIEWS OF CHILDREN AND THEIR ATTITUDES TO PHYSICAL EDUCATION

Aims: 1. To introduce means of gathering data by administered questionnaires.
2. To examine the connections between children's attitudes to physical activity and the planning of the curriculum of Physical Education.

Introduction

In this project, we move from the pre-determined, open-ended, semi-structured, exploratory questionnaire design, to a more highly structured interview schedule where responses are predetermined. Whereas in the previous project the interviewer was responsible for recording the verbal answers of the interviewee, in this project, the interviewee is expected to record his own answers to pre-determined questions. Obviously, each person could be interviewed personally to ensure unambiguity of response, but this would be time-consuming and would limit the number of people who could be interviewed. Questionnaires can be administered in schools by the researcher or by the teacher to large groups of children providing the instructions are clear and unambiguous, the list of questions is not too long and time-consuming, and the children are assured of anonymity so preventing biased or incomplete questionnaires. Questionnaires could be sent to children, a strategy which captures a wider population but would lead to a reduced return and pose problems which would affect the reliability of the evidence. This type of administered questionnaire reduces interviewer bias by asking the same questions in the same words and allows the responses to be accurately compared through a system of coding the answers. This project is also hypothesis testing for the same reasons that were offered in the previous study and two hypotheses have been devised. Obviously, the number of hypotheses will depend upon the nature of the problem being studied.

Study Area

Teachers of physical education are aware that an effective teaching programme will depend upon a number of factors including the children's positive attitude towards the subject. These attitudes are acquired both inside and outside schools from parents and friends as well as from teachers. Allport[1] has described attitude as:

a mental and neural state of readiness, organized through experience exerting a directive or dynamic influence upon the individual's response to all objects and situations with which it is related.

Attitude, therefore, can be inferred from what a person says or does. An individual's response towards an object is also a compound of what he knows or believes about it, how he feels about it, and what he is inclined to do about it. These three components of attitudes towards physical education—the cognitive, affective and behavioural—reveal themselves in different ways. Cognitive components are revealed in terms of verbal statements of knowledge and beliefs, affective in verbal statements of likes and dislikes, and behaviour in terms of verbal statements of how a person intends to act in relation to physical education. In this project, the affective component is being analysed.

In setting out to study attitudes towards physical education, it would be too simplistic to imagine that all forms of physical education will be perceived as providing equal sources of satisfaction or dissatisfaction amongst all boys and girls. In fact, from a review of literature it can be hypothesised that, in part, physical education exists for social, health, ascetic, vertigo, recreation, competition and aesthetic purposes[2]. Part of this project, therefore, will investigate the attitudes of school children to these seven sub-dimensions.

However, these dispositions towards physical education vary from individual to individual and group to group, partly as a reflection of a person's unique personality structure and partly as a result of his previous experience. A positive or negative attitude to physical education, therefore, may vary from child to child or from group to group in different social settings. In schools, there is evidence to suggest that children from higher socio-economic groups have a more positive attitude to physical education than those from lower socio-economic groups; that children in selective schools have a more positive attitude than children from non-selective schools; that children in higher streams will have a more positive attitude than children in lower streams; that boys in general have a more positive attitude to physical education than girls; and that younger children have a more positive attitude to physical education than older children[3]. The last two factors have been isolated for study here and the following hypotheses are proposed.

Hypotheses

1. In secondary schools, boys will have a more positive attitude towards physical education than girls, and
2. Younger pupils will have a more positive attitude towards physical education than older pupils.

Procedure

Questionnaire Design
Procedures can be devised to formulate a number of questions to determine a person's attitude towards physical education[4]. Briefly, the steps adopted to formulate the attitude questionnaire used in this project were as follows:

A group of children was asked to describe what they liked and disliked about physical education in relation to the seven dimensions described earlier. A questionnaire consisting of seventy items was then devised. To ensure that the pupils could not differentiate between the seven dimensions in the scale the questions were listed in strict rotation so that each dimension appeared at every seventh interval.

A Likert scale was adopted to measure intensity of response to each item in the questionnaire so that in answer to any one question the children would 'strongly agree,' 'agree,' 'disagree' or 'strongly disagree.' For instance, in relation to the question 'social dancing is good fun,' the response could be one of four from 'strongly agree' through to 'strongly disagree.' These responses were given a score of one to four marks with four marks being allocated to 'strongly agree.' To provide variety, some questions were posed in reverse order.

A pilot study was conducted to eliminate questions which did not produce a wide range of responses; to ensure that each question could be easily understood; and to test the practicability of the procedures for administering the questionnaire.

The questionnaire was then administered to selected groups of children.

Administration of the Questionnaire

Two modes of testing have been devised in this project. The first necessitates the collection and analysis of the results of a questionnaire administered by students to selected groups of children. The second requires the analysis of raw scores which have been collected from the results of a study of first and fourth year boys and girls[5]. All students should be aware of the procedures of testing which are outlined[6].

Exercises

The exercises outlined below have been devised to obtain a broad picture of differences of attitude. Obviously, an appraisal of differences between and within sub-domains would produce a more comprehensive and detailed record of other factors involved in defining children's attitudes to physical education.

Mode One
1. Test all boys and girls in the first and fourth years of a secondary school (APPENDIX I).
2. Record the result.

Modes One and Two
3. By means of a critical ratio test, compare the differences in attitude between
   (a) all boys and all girls
   (b) all first year pupils and all fourth year pupils (APPENDIX II).
4. Analyse the results in relation to the hypotheses.
5. Discuss the implications of the results of this study for the planning of the curriculum of physical education in schools.
6. Compare the results with the results of another study outlined in the bibliography.

Notes and Bibliography

(1) ALLPORT, G.W. Quoted in N. Warren & M. Jahoda. (1973). (Eds.). "Attitudes". Harmondsworth: Penguin. 24.

(2) A review of relevant literature can be found in:

LOY, J.W. & KENYON, G.S. (Eds.). "Sport, Culture and Society". London: Macmillan. 44-81.

(3) For example:

ABEL, G. & KNAPP, B. (1967). Physical activity interests of secondary schoolgirls. *Bull. of Phys. Educ.,* **7**, 4-15.

COWELL, C.C. (1973). The contribution of physical activity to social development. In J.A. Mangan (Ed.). "Physical Education and Sport: Sociological and Cultural Perspectives". Oxford: Blackwell.

CRUNDEN, C.C. (1970). Sport and social background: a study of 13 and 15 year old children. *Bull. of Phys. Educ.,* **8**, 36-40.

DALE, R.R. (1974). "Mixed or Single-Sex School". London: Routledge and Kegan Paul. 170-183.

EMMETT, I. (1971). "Youth and Leisure in an Urban Sprawl". Manchester: University Press. 17-28, 44-54.

HARGREAVES, D.H. (1967). "Social Relations in a Secondary School". London: Routledge and Kegan Paul. 68-82.

JACKSON, B. & MARSDEN, D. (1966). "Education and the Working Class". Harmondsworth: Penguin. 119-129.

KING, R. (1969). Values and Involvement in the Grammar School. London: Routledge and Kegan Paul. 72-99, 113-132.

LAMBERT, R. & MILLHAM, S. (1968). "The Hothouse Society". Harmondsworth: Pelican.

ROCHE, A.G. (1965). Attitude testing in physical education with 14-15 year old boys. Carnegie College of Physical Education: *Research Papers in Physical Education,* **1**, 29-37.

WARD, E., HARDMAN, K. & ALMOND, L. (1968). Investigation into the problem of participation and attitudes to physical activity of 11-18 year old boys. *Research in Physical Education,* **1**, 18-26.

WHITE, G.B., WHITELEY, G., VENTRE, A.G.L. & MASON, M.G. (1965). Attitude to athletics of second and fourth year boys in secondary schools. Carnegie College of Physical Education: *Research Papers in Physical Education,* **1**, 51-54.

(4) ADAMS, R.S. (1963). Two scales for measuring attitude towards physical education. *Res. Quart.,* **34**, 91-94.

KEOGH, J. (1962). Extreme attitudes towards physical education. *Res. Quart.,* **34**, 27-33.

(5) SAUNDERS, C. (1974). An investigation of secondary school children's attitude to physical education in school. New University of Ulster: Dip. Adv. St. of Educ.

(6) OPPENHEIM, A.N. (1966). "Questionnaire Design and Attitude Measurement". London: Heinemann.

Appendix I Instructions for Answering the Questionnaire

YEAR: CLASS:

GIRL/BOY   (Cross out that which does not apply)

INTRODUCTION

The following enquiry has been designed to find out how boys and girls perceive *physical education in schools.* I am asking you to tell me what you think and feel about *physical education.* The best answer is *your own personal opinion.*

INSTRUCTIONS

1. Express your agreement or disagreement by circling the letters at the left-hand side of each statement according to the following:

    SA : strongly agree
     A : agree
     D : disagree
    SD : strongly disagree

For example if you *strongly disagree* with a statement, circle the letters SD as follows:

SA   A   D   (SD)   (a) PE in schools is a waste of time.

2. Work on your own.

3. Reply to all statements in *THE ORDER GIVEN.*

4. Do not spend too much time on any one statement; read it, circle a letter or letters and go on to the next.

DO NOT OPEN THE BOOKLET UNTIL YOU ARE TOLD TO DO SO

Instructions for Administering the Questionnaire

1. Distribute the questionnaires to all the boys and girls in the class and read through the instructions on the front page very carefully.
2. Ask if there are any queries.
3. Remind subjects to work on their own

    answer every question in order
    give their personal opinion
    work quickly.

4. Collect all the questionnaires.

The questionnaire.

SA A D SD	1.	Physical education helps to keep me free from illness.
SA A D SD	2.	I always feel annoyed when we lose a match.
SA A D SD	3.	You make more new friends through sport than through any other activity.
SA A D SD	4.	In the gym I prefer climbing and swinging on the ropes to floor exercises.
SA A D SD	5R*	Activities which are done on the spur of the moment are much more enjoyable than those which receive long periods of practice.
SA A D SD	6.	It is good to have a PE lesson after sitting in classes all morning.
SA A D SD	7.	I get great pleasure from moving well.
SA A D SD	8.	I like doing Keep Fit exercises in PE because they make me feel fit and healthy.
SA A D SD	9.	Winning a game makes me feel happy and content.
SA A D SD	10.	I like to take part in physical activities where I mix with other people.
SA A D SD	11.	I would rather spend a swimming lesson jumping and diving into the water than just swimming around.
SA A D SD	12.	I like taking part in practices where I can see my performance improve.
SA A D SD	13.	It is more relaxing to play a game than read a book.
SA A D SD	14R	I am not interested in making my gym or dance movements look beautiful.
SA A D SD	15.	I think it is important to have a strong, healthy body.
SA A D SD	16.	I like playing in class matches at school.
SA A D SD	17.	PE lessons are friendly and enjoyable when we work in groups.

*R = reverse order coding. This symbol does not appear on the pupils' questionnaire.

SA A D SD	18. I always want to take part when I watch trampolining.
SA A D SD	19. The only way to play a game well is to put a lot of hard work into the practice.
SA A D SD	20. There is nothing like a good game of netball or football to take your mind off your work.
SA A D SD	21. I love to see Olympic gymnastics on TV because the movements are so pleasing to watch.
SA A D SD	22. I feel fit and healthy after doing PE.
SA A D SD	23. You should always play games to win.
SA A D SD	24. Social dancing is good fun.
SA A D SD	25. I like taking part in dangerous games and sports
SA A D SD	26R Activities are not worth doing when you have to spend a lot of time practising.
SA A D SD	27. If I had the chance, I would visit the gym in my free time as often as I could.
SA A D SD	28. I think some footballers move well when they have the ball.
SA A D SD	29. Being physically fit is very important to me.
SA A D SD	30. I always try hard to win even in practice games at school.
SA A D SD	31. I like PE lessons when we choose the groups we want to work in.
SA A D SD	32. I would rather work on the top beam in the gym than on the bottom beam.
SA A D SD	33R I do not like athletics in school because it takes too much time practising in order to improve.
SA A D SD	34. Practically the only way to 'let off steam' is through some form of physical activity.
SA A D SD	35. Dance lessons in school give me the opportunity to feel graceful and beautiful when I move.
SA A D SD	36R The time spent in PE doing vigorous exercises could be used better in other ways.
SA A D SD	37. The score is always important when you play games.
SA A D SD	38. One of the best ways of getting to know people is through joining a sports club.
SA A D SD	39. I think ski jumping is thrilling and exciting to watch.
SA A D SD	40. It is necessary to practise skills if you want to play a game better.
SA A D SD	41R When I'm not working I would rather watch TV than play a game.
SA A D SD	42R The idea that every human movement is graceful is stupid.
SA A D SD	43R It is not important to have a strong, fit and healthy body.
SA A D SD	44. It is important to win in matches against other schools.
SA A D SD	45R Playing games can sometimes spoil good friendships.
SA A D SD	46. I like taking part in physical activities that are dangerous and exciting.
SA A D SD	47R I like doing physical activities that do not require a lot of practising.
SA A D SD	48. Physical activities should take up most of our leisure time.
SA A D SD	49R Too much time is spent in gym lessons on making our movements look good.
SA A D SD	50R I think it is a waste of time to develop strong, healthy muscles.
SA A D SD	51R I only like to play games when the result does not matter.
SA A D SD	52. I met my best friends through games and sports.
SA A D SD	53. I like movements in the gym where I have to leave the floor.
SA A D SD	54R Learning physical skills such as throwing, tackling, dodging and marking are boring.
SA A D SD	55R Most mental activities are just as relaxing as physical ones.
SA A D SD	56. I think activities such as diving, trampolining and skating are beautiful to watch.
SA A D SD	57R I do not like fitness training lessons in PE.

SA A D SD   58R The match is important, not whether you win or lose.
SA A D SD   59R In school I do not like physical activities that involve mixing with other people.
SA A D SD   60.   In school I enjoy playing those games where there is some risk to my safety.
SA A D SD   61.   Practising is necessary for better performance.
SA A D SD   62.   A game of basketball or tennis is the best way to 'let yourself go' after a morning in the classroom.
SA A D SD   63.   I love to watch a footballer making a running leap to head the ball into the back of the net.
SA A D SD   64R PE lessons are spoiled when the emphasis is on strength and fitness.
SA A D SD   65.   PE lessons are great when you compete against other teams.
SA A D SD   66R I like working by myself in the PE lesson.
SA A D SD   67.   I like movements in the gym where I feel my body 'whizzing' through the air.
SA A D SD   68.   I would gladly undergo the months of hard and exhausting training necessary to make an Olympic team, football team or the hockey team.
SA A D SD   69.   I forget all my problems when I'm playing games.
SA A D SD   70.   I enjoy watching the style of a high diver.

Appendix II Raw Scores

First year Boys (N=40)		First year Girls (N=40)		Fourth year Boys (N=40)		Fourth year Girls (N=40)	
208	216	190	194	194	216	184	193
175	183	198	210	182	212	212	210
212	162	195	162	188	197	206	196
235	209	163	183	232	186	186	212
203	209	169	193	186	233	189	232
190	220	189	188	171	232	145	203
223	227	210	203	183	159	149	197
226	221	195	183	197	183	178	214
198	239	196	225	189	176	176	205
200	204	207	213	187	217	192	241
185	234	204	222	191	201	212	212
227	235	187	183	184	191	213	188
222	238	188	173	217	222	202	188
201	239	216	214	208	198	190	169
208	247	202	189	180	168	146	209
219	134	169	193	178	209	215	183
200	211	203	200	179	201	191	161
205	178	238	184	218	208	189	193
188	206	183	216	181	193	203	174
214	189	205	177	168	227	197	181

Part 6   Experimental
Situations

Project 11

LEADERSHIP INFLUENCE IN AN EXPERIMENTAL SITUATION

Aims: 1. To construct an experimental situation in which groups are involved in the performance of certain simple physical tasks either against time or to achieve a score.
2. To introduce into this situation group leaders operating in three different styles and to observe and record the effects of such leadership upon group interaction and performance.

Introduction

Of the many interesting characteristics of group interaction the process by which leadership develops is perhaps the most complex[1].

In considering leadership as a phenomenon of group life, it is important to recognize the distinction between formal and informal groupings. When people enter an institution such as a school or college or become part of a military or civil organization it is usual for them to be grouped for the purpose of instruction or administration. The persons concerned have little or no choice over the membership, or the size of the formal group to which they are allocated. An informal group, on the other hand, will develop because several individuals wish to be members for a variety of reasons, such as sharing the same beliefs or interests, or having a common task or goal. Both types of group will have at least one leader. In the formal group the leader will be appointed; in the informal group a leader will emerge as the result of interaction between the group members. In both cases, however, the leader will be concerned with, or instrumental in, satisfying the socio-emotional needs of the group he leads and in the achievement of the goal or task.

The way in which the leader operates has been termed his leadership style and this is the subject of a classic experiment by Lippitt and White.[2] These investigators defined three styles of leadership—authoritarian, democratic and laissez-faire—and recorded the effects of each different style upon the work, relationships, attitude and behaviour of eleven year old boys in club groups over a period of 21 weekly meetings. Their observations showed that the demands made upon the leader by the group varied with the style adopted and that the styles differed in their effects on morale (socio-emotional area) and work done (task effectiveness).

Study Area

The subject of physical education has concerned itself as much with methodology as with content and philosophy. It is not surprising, therefore, that the teacher of physical education has been preoccupied with the methods that are available for his use—a preoccupation that has at times led him to the acceptance of innovations on methodological rather than philosophical grounds. The need for a study of strategies and methods available to the teacher of physical education is reinforced, however, by the complexity of the subject including, as it does, such different activities as major team games and outdoor activities; a wide range of age and ability even within a school setting for which the teacher must be prepared; and the many situations from the compulsory, timetabled lesson to the voluntary, after-school club in which the teacher will be required to play a different role.

That the teacher is the formal leader of his class is disputed more openly and frequently at present than in the past for reasons which are discussed by Hargreaves[3] among others. In such circumstances, the teacher's effectiveness may depend as much upon the style he adopts as upon his personality and knowledge of his subject. An examination of three different styles of leadership is not in itself adequate to describe teaching effectiveness but may initially be illustrative of some simple aspects of a more complex whole.

Procedure

1. Students are required to observe, record and participate in an experimental situation which focuses attention upon the task effectiveness of three small groups in the performance of basketball skills under authoritarian, democratic and laissez-faire styles of leadership.

2. Three groups of three or four members each should be selected either randomly or equated in terms of basketball ability. A leader should be appointed for each group. (A member of the experimental team appointed to lead each group would facilitate pre- and post-experimental discussion and ensure that the styles were accurately portrayed. Such an arrangement would result in equal teams of four or five). The leaders should each receive one of the 'letters' shown at APPENDIX I. The team members should not see the 'letters' or be aware of their content.

3. Recorders/Administrators need to be appointed as follows:
   A. A general co-ordinator who will:
      i) regulate the movement of the groups to each activity in turn. Each group will remain at its allocated activity until requested to move to the next. All groups will move to a new activity at the same time and a stop clock/watch, visible to all the group (interaction) recorders, will be restarted from zero on the order to move.
      ii) record on a master recording sheet (APPENDIX II) all the necessary information for later examination and analysis, the scorer for each task reporting at the end of each group's attempt.
   B. Three group interaction recorders (one for each group) who will:
      i) record all verbal interaction of the groups for which they are responsible on interaction recording sheets (APPENDICES III A, B and

           c). (If numbered vests or bibs of three different colours are worn by the members of the three groups this greatly aids the recorders in their task).

      ii) note, for their groups, by referring to the main stop clock/watch, the time taken on each task between receiving the order to move and the first shot, run, throw etc., that is, the discussion/organization time.

  C. Five timekeepers/scorers (one for each of the basketball tasks)* who will:

      i) hand the card bearing details of their task (APPENDIX IV) to the group leader on arrival at the new task station after the order to move.

      ii) record accurately and impartially, the time taken or score made (as specified on the card). No assistance or direction should be given other than that concerning the correct form of the task. This recorded score/time should be handed over to the general co-ordinator confidentially.

      iii) assist the general co-ordinator by holding each group at his task station until ordered to move.

  D. The gymnasium should be set out with necessary apparatus and chalked lines as shown in the plan at APPENDIX V.

Exercises

1. a) On the master recording sheet score each group three points if they came first on a task, two points if they were second and one point if they were third.
   b) Total the discussion/organization time for each group.
2. a) Which group scored highest over the five tasks?
   b) What style of leadership were the members subjected to?
   c) Which group proved least effective, that is, produced the lowest score over the five tasks?
   d) What style of leadership operated in this group?
3. a) Which group had the highest total discussion/organization time?
   b) Which group had the lowest total discussion/organization time?
   c) Under what style of leadership did these groups operate?
4. a) Which group had the most verbal interaction during the completion of the tasks?
   b) Which group had the least verbal interaction during the completion of the tasks.
   c) Under what style of leadership did these groups operate?
5. Consider the group members' reactions to the style of leadership under which they operated. What feelings did they have about their leader? Was his contribution to the group's effort positive? (that is, apart from his own score, did his leadership contribute anything?)
6. Assuming that each group began equal, did any group do much worse, or much better, than they felt they should have done? What might account for such an occurrence?
7. Within the limitations of this experiment discuss the implications of the three different styles of leadership for the role of the physical education teacher.

*If five timekeepers/scorers are not available it is possible to use three, each allocated to one group and moving with the group from one task to the next.

Notes and Bibliography

(1) A useful collection of theoretical and empirical studies can be found in:
   GIBB, C.A. (1969). "Leadership". Harmondsworth: Penguin.
(2) LIPPITT, R. & WHITE, R.K. (1952). An Experimental Study of Leadership and Group Life. In G.E.
   Swanson, T.M. Newcomb & E.L. Hartley (Eds.). "Readings in Social Psychology." New York: Holt.
(3) HARGREAVES, D.H. (1967). "Social Relations in a Secondary School". London: Routledge. 171-174.
   Additional sources of information can be found in:
   BANKS, O. (1968). "The Sociology of Education". London: Batsford. 180-188.
   BROOKOVER, W.B. & GOTTLIEB, B. (1964). "A Sociology of Education". New York: American Book Co.
   423-452.
   HOYLE, E. (1969). "The Role of the Teacher". London: Routledge and Kegan Paul. 58-68.
   SHIPMAN, M.D. (1968). "Sociology of the School". London: Longmans. 136-147.

Appendix 1

PLEASE AVOID DISCUSSING THE CONTENT OF THIS NOTE WITH ANYONE ELSE. IT WILL DEFEAT THE PURPOSE OF THE EXERCISE.

I want you to be the leader of a group. The group task will be to perform some basketball skills for speed and accuracy and your group's score will be compared with the scores of other groups.

I want you and your group to do as well as possible but I want you to adopt the role of *laissez-faire* leader.

You must not try to organize the group in any way nor direct their efforts. If suggestions are made by any of the group members neither accept nor reject them . . . . . be very non-committal. 'We don't need to do things in any special way.' Be passive in your approach to leadership of the group rather than active.

Let them get on with things in their own way and you concentrate on your own personal contribution to the group task. However, try to avoid letting anyone else assume the role of leader.

PLEASE AVOID DISCUSSING THE CONTENTS OF THIS NOTE WITH ANYONE ELSE. IT WILL DEFEAT THE PURPOSE OF THE EXERCISE.

I want you to be the leader of a group. The group task will be to perform some basketball skills for speed and accuracy and your group's score will be compared with the scores of other groups.

I want you and your group to do as well as possible but I want you to adopt the role of *democratic* leader.

Don't give orders; make suggestions. For example, 'Let's try it this way.' . . . . . 'Let's do what so-and-so suggests'.

Receive suggestions from the rest of the group and, even go so far as to invite suggestions. Try to get everyone involved in what has to be done.

Be tolerant but sufficiently firm in your approach to make it appear that you are the leader of the group without being dogmatic or dictatorial.

PLEASE AVOID DISCUSSING THE CONTENTS OF THIS NOTE WITH ANYONE ELSE. IT WILL DEFEAT THE PURPOSE OF THE EXERCISE.

I want you to be the leader of a group. The group task will be to perform some basketball skills for speed and accuracy and your group's score will be compared with the scores of other groups.

I want you and your group to do as well as possible but I want you to adopt the role of *authoritarian* leader.

There is only one way to do things and that is your way and everyone else should conform. Give orders not advice. Other people's suggestions should be over-ruled.

Insist on a strict order and discipline.

Try to act only in accordance with your interpretation of authoritarian leadership.

Appendix II

MASTER RECORDING SHEET

	Task 1		Task 2		Task 3		Task 4		Task 5		Total time taken before work begins	Total of rank orders	Total working time
	Score / Rank	Organization time	Score / Rank	Organization time	Score / Rank	Organization time	Score / Rank	Organization time	Score / Rank	Organization time			
Group A													
Group B													
Group C													

Appendix IIIA

INTERACTION RECORD Group	Task 1	Task 2	Task 3	Task 4	Task 5	Total Verbal Inter- action
Name Number						
Total verbal interaction on each task						
Time taken to organize and begin work						

1. In the appropriate row and column record with a tick (√) each time a member of the team speaks.
2. Record the time that elapses between the order to move to the new task and the commencement of the first shot, run, throw etc.

Appendix IIIB

INTERACTION RECORD Group	Task 1	Task 2	Task 3	Task 4	Task 5	Total Verbal Inter-action
Name Number						
Total verbal interaction on each task						
Time taken to organize and begin work						

1. In the appropriate row and column record with a tick (√) each time a member of the team speaks.
2. Record the time that elapses between the order to move to the new task and the commencement of the first shot, run, throw etc.

Appendix IIIC

INTERACTION RECORD Group	Task 1	Task 2	Task 3	Task 4	Task 5	Total Verbal Inter-action
Name Number						
Total verbal interaction on each task						
Time taken to organize and begin work						

1. In the appropriate row and column record with a tick (√) each time a member of the team speaks.
2. Record the time that elapses between the order to move to the new task and the commencement of the first shot, run, throw etc.

Appendix IV

Task No. 1

All members of the group must work in turn.

One ball only is available.

Starting behind the bench each member dribbles forward to take a lay-up shot at the basket.

When you are ready to begin inform the scorer so that he can start the stop-watch. The total number of baskets made by the group in TWO minutes will be recorded.

Only baskets which conform to the conditions of this task will be counted.

Task No. 2

All members of the group must work in turn.

One ball only is available.

When the group is ready inform the scorer so that he can start the stop-watch.

Begin behind the line. Dribble across the gym to make a lay-up shot against the far wall, collect the rebound, dribble back and make a lay-up shot against the near wall, collect the rebound and pass the ball to the next group member.

The group must go twice each and the total time taken will be recorded.

The watch cannot be stopped for errors!

Task No. 3

All members of the group must work in turn.

One ball only is available.

When the group is ready to begin inform the scorer so that he can start the stop-watch.

The task is for each member of the group to pass the ball from a position behind the bench to hit the four targets on the wall in turn collecting the rebound himself after each pass.

The time taken by the whole group will be recorded.

A time limit of TWO minutes and THIRTY seconds will operate.

Task No. 4

Two balls are available for this task.

When the group is ready to begin inform the scorer so that he can start the stop-watch.

The objective is for each member of the group to have TWO shots at basket from each of the three marked positions.

The number of successful baskets will be recorded, but any scored from incorrect positions will be ignored.

A maximum time limit of TWO minutes and THIRTY seconds will operate.

Task No. 5

All members of the group must work in turn.

One ball only is available.

When the group is ready to begin inform the scorer so that he can start the stop-watch.

Starting behind the line, dribble the ball zig-zag fashion in and out of the obstacles to the end of the line and back again. Hand the ball to the next member of the group only when you have passed the last obstacle.

The whole group must go twice.

The time will be recorded from starting to when the last man hands the ball to the first man after the group has completed two runs each.

The watch cannot be stopped for errors!

Appendix V   Plan of Gymnasium for Basketball Tasks

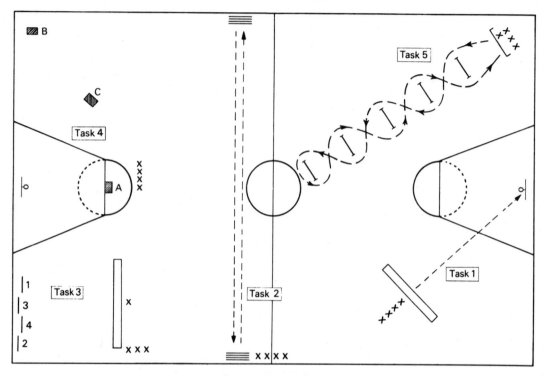

TASK 1   A bench placed about 18–20 feet from the basket behind which the group members stand prior to taking their turn. One basketball and one stopwatch.

TASK 2   A target (chalk cross or coloured braid looped onto top wall-bar) for a lay-up shot at each side of the gymnasium. One ball and one stopwatch.

TASK 3   A bench placed about 12–15 feet away from a blank wall or window ladder with four targets marked in chalk and numbered one to four. One ball and one stopwatch. (The targets might be 15–18 inches square.)

TASK 4   Three targets marked on the floor in positions similar to those shown on the above plan and clearly lettered. Two balls and one stopwatch.

TASK 5   Four or five chairs (beam saddles or hurdles) placed at suitable intervals in a straight line from the restraining line for a zig-zag dribble. One ball and one stopwatch.

THE TASK CARDS BEARING INSTRUCTIONS SHOULD BE PLACED FACE DOWN ON THE BENCH AT THE START OF EACH ACTIVITY OR LEFT IN POSSESSION OF THE TIMEKEEPER/SCORER AND HANDED TO THE GROUP LEADER ON A SIGNAL FROM THE CO-ORDINATOR.

Project 12

CONFLICT AND COMPETITION IN AN EXPERIMENTAL SITUATION IN A TEAM GAME

Aims: 1. To structure a situation in which small groups are involved in a competitive team game.
2. To introduce factors designed to create intra-group competition and conflict and to observe and record the effects of these factors upon performance and verbal and symbolic interaction.

Introduction

In his study and observation of group behaviour the sociologist has noted that persons associate in groups in order to achieve common goals, satisfy needs which they share (for example for affection and affiliation) or because of common beliefs, standards or values. It might be inferred, therefore, that the climate or condition within the group would be co-operative. Since they share the same goal, needs, beliefs and standards the members would co-operate with one another in order to achieve their ends. Such a view oversimplifies the situation as it exists in reality for man learns at a very early age that some of his needs or goals can best be achieved by competitive behaviour and also that an intensified form of intra-group competition leads to conflict, for example, over who is boss of his gang.

These conditions of co-operation, competition and conflict have been accurately and intelligibly defined by Merrill[1]. Co-operation 'is a form of social interaction wherein two or more persons (or groups) work together for a common end,' whereas, 'in competition the end sought can only be achieved by some but not all of the individuals.' Conflict is 'a situation of competition in which the parties are aware of the incompatibility of potential future positions and in which each party wishes to occupy a position that is incompatible with the wishes of the other.'

Some authorities have viewed society and group life purely in terms of one of the three conditions defined above. In describing the conflict model of society Mills[2] portrays conflict as an important dynamic force, the resolution of which brings about beneficial changes in society only in turn to create new strains to be resolved by further changes and so on.

It is difficult to find any situations in real life which are entirely described by one of the definitions above. Almost all are combinations of those conditions even though when there is more observed evidence of one than the others it is convenient to use that name to describe it. Elias and Dunning[3] have referred to this in their approach to the dynamics of a game of football as 'controlled tensions.'

The sociologist's interest in these conditions operating within groups has been to discover how they originate, how they operate and their effects upon the group. In this project, an attempt is made to generate the conditions artificially, to observe and discuss in general terms how they operate in the practical work and to discover the effects they have upon performance and interaction.

Study Area

A great number of activities in physical education are competitive in nature or may be so organized as to promote competition between individuals or groups. Another type of organization involving attempts to achieve or improve upon a score or standard (recorded by the same or another group on a previous occasion) permits, what has been termed, indirect competition. This project is not concerned primarily with either of these sorts of competition though viewed in a general way they would illustrate the conditions and forces which may be operating when competition or conflict develops within a group. It is this which is the specific concern of this project.

Whilst competition may play a part in determining the composition of the team it is normally one of the teacher/coach's aims to reduce intra-group conflict and/or competition to a minimum. This is attempted in the hope of achieving maximum co-operation between the members and promoting group cohesion for, as Lenk[4] has stated, 'For group achievement, internal competition would be inhibitory.'

Lenk's own study of the German national rowing eights supports a contrary view, namely, that the teams in question could achieve success and maintain performances at the highest possible level in spite of marked internal conflicts so that he concludes, 'The thesis that only low conflict groups can achieve high levels of performance is not generally valid.'

Procedure

1. The basis for the experimental work is a round robin tournament involving three teams in playing games of hockey (5—8 a side) or basketball (5 a side). The teams needed to be equated for number, ability and composition, that is, in mixed teams of the same proportion of men and women.

2. Each team will play under a different internal condition. These conditions will be artificially induced but may be sufficiently realistic and long-lasting enough for the effects upon interaction and performance to be observed.

3. The members of Team A should each receive a copy of the note to be found at APPENDIX IA; the members of Team B a copy of the note at APPENDIX IB; and the members of Team C a copy of the note at APPENDIX IC. These should be given to individuals, preferably in advance (say 12 hours), and treated as confidential.
   (An alternative form of note IC is shown at APPENDIX ID, which would be suitable for distribution to the female members of a mixed hockey team).

4. The tournament should now take place, each game being played for between five

and ten minutes each way (hockey on a pitch of suitable dimensions for the size of team).

The following order of play is suggested.

Team A versus Team C

Team B versus Team C

Team A versus Team B

The experiment might be improved (numbers and time permitting) by the inclusion of a fourth (control) team who receive no instructions. It might then run

(a) A v B   (c) A v D   (e) A v C

(b) C v D   (d) C v B   (f) B v D

5. The following officials and recorders should be appointed:
   (a) for the games
        a referee
        a scorer, and
        a timekeeper
   (b) Two recorders (or two pairs of recorders) to each active team. The same recorders can be used to observe Teams B and C in the second game as have observed A and C respectively in the first game. They will be responsible for recording all verbal and symbolic interaction in the games which take place on the recording sheets to be found at APPENDIX IIA and B.
        N.B. Their task will be made very much easier if numbered bibs are available in a different colour for each team.

Exercises

1. Which team scored most goals/baskets during the tournament? Which team conceded fewest goals/baskets during the tournament? What internal conditions were induced in these teams? Do these results support Lenk's proposition? What other factors may have influenced the results in this experiment?
2. Which team made the greatest number of passes? What condition had been induced? Which team made fewest passes? Does the number of passes made by a team vary greatly according to the opposition? (A more detailed analysis by teams taking each game in turn should be attempted here with discussion of factors which may be relevant).
3. Taking each team in turn, which individual made the most passes? Which individual made the least passes? Is there a marked divergence or convergence in the number of passes made by individuals under the different internal conditions?
4. Repeat tasks of Exercise 2 above relating now to verbal interaction.
5. Repeat tasks of Exercise 3 above relating now to verbal interaction.
6. Discuss the implications of these findings in relation to the organization and teaching of games in school.

Notes and Bibliography

(1) MERRILL, F.E. (1965). Society and Culture. London: Prentice Hall. 32-35.
(2) MILLS, T.M. (1967). The Sociology of Small Groups. London: Prentice Hall. 14-15.
(3) ELIAS, N. & DUNNING, E. (1966). Dynamics of Group Sport with Special Reference to Football. *B.J. Sociol.*, 14, 388-402.
(4) LENK, H. (1969). Top Performance Despite Internal Conflict. In J.W. Loy & G.S. Kenyon. (Eds.). Sport, Culture and Society. New York: McMillan.

Appendix IA

PLEASE AVOID DISCUSSING THE CONTENTS OF THIS NOTE WITH ANYONE ELSE.

The observers are looking for the best *team* play.
> They will be influenced by which side wins the game and by:
>> the way individuals play together as a team;
>> the way you personally co-operate with other players, as well as looking for
>> unselfishness in the way individuals play.
> Selfishness and ball-hogging will be counted as very unfavourable behaviour.
> Remember that it is the team that counts . . . not the individual.
> Do all you can to make your team successful even if it means that you don't get into the score sheet.

Appendix IB

PLEASE AVOID DISCUSSING THE CONTENTS OF THIS NOTE WITH ANYONE ELSE.

The observers are looking for:
> the best individual player;
> the person who scores the most goals/baskets;
> the person who works hardest in both attack and defence;
> the number of times a player makes an important contribution to the game.

Remember, if you are to be seen to best advantage, you must take all the chances you are given and make as many chances for yourself as possible. If you don't make them no-one else will!!!
If someone else is rated best in any of these aspects of play it means that you can't be !!!

Appendix IC

PLEASE AVOID DISCUSSING THE CONTENTS OF THIS NOTE WITH ANYONE ELSE.

The observers are here to decide who would be the best person to act as captain of this team.
> They will be influenced by such things as your own part in the game and the tactical knowledge and judgement you show during the game. Taking a leading part in initiating team patterns of play is also likely to be regarded as a positive sign of captaincy potential.
> Try to ensure by your actions that the observers are in no doubt by the end of play that you are the best candidate for the captaincy and don't be afraid to let your team mates see that you mean to be boss. (It is doubtful if they know as much about the game as you do anyway!)

Appendix ID

PLEASE AVOID DISCUSSING THE CONTENTS OF THIS NOTE WITH ANYONE ELSE.

The observers are here to decide who should be the best person to act as captain.

Because this is a mixed team one of the men will probably think that he is automatically the person for the captain's position.

Just show him and the observers that you know as much about the game, its rules and tactics as he does and that you are not prepared to be dictated to by him.

Appendix IIA

First Half   Second Half

When a player passes the ball write the number of the player to whom he passes in the passer's row on the score sheet.

At the end calculate: Who made the most passes? Who made the least passes?

Who received the most passes? Who received the least passes?

What was the total number of passes made by the team in each game and overall?

N.B. The recorders will require one of these sheets for each team for each game.

Appendix IIB

First Half   Second Half

When a player speaks to another, write that player's number in the speaker's row on the scoresheet. Use a tick if someone speaks but not to anyone in particular; an 'R' if he speaks to the referee and a player's number with a ring round it if he speaks to a player of the opposition. At the end calculate: Who spoke most often? Who was spoken to most?
Who spoke least? Who was spoken to least?
The total number of times a person spoke during each game and overall.

N.B. The recorders will require one of these sheets for each team for each game.

BIBLIOGRAPHY

ABEL, G. & KNAPP, B. (1967). Physical activity interests of secondary schoolgirls. *Bull. of Phys. Educ.*, 7, 4-15.

ABRAHAMS, M. (1966). Testing consumer demand in sport. *Sport & Recreation.* 7, 32-36.

ADAMS, R.S. (1963). Two scales for measuring attitude towards physical education. *Res. Quart.*, 34, 91-94.

ANDERSON, N. (1961). "Work and Leisure". London: Routledge and Kegan Paul.

ARGYLE, M. (1973). "Social Encounters". Harmondsworth: Penguin.

AVEDON, E.M. & SUTTON-SMITH, B. (1971). "The Study of Games". London: Wiley.

BANKS, O. (1955). "Parity and Prestige in English Secondary Education". London: Routledge and Kegan Paul.

BANKS, O. (1968). "The Sociology of Education". London: Batsford.

BANKS, O. & FINLAYSON, D. (1973). "Success and Failure in the Secondary School". London: Methuen.

BERELSON, B. (1971). "Content Analysis in Communication Research". New York: Hafner.

BERNSTEIN, B. (1972). Sociology and sociology of education: some aspects. In "School and Society Unit 17". Bletchley: The Open University Press.

BIDWELL, C.E. (1965). The school as a formal organisation. In J.G. March. (Ed.). "Handbook of Organisations". Chicago: Rand McNally.

BIRCH, J.G. (1971). "Indoor Sports Centres". Sports Council Studies 1. London: H.M.S.O.

BROOKOVER, W.B. & GOTTLIEB, B. (1964). "A Sociology of Education". New York: American Book Co.

BURROUGHS, G.E.R. (1971). "Design and Analysis in Educational Research". Birmingham: University of Birmingham Monograph No. 8.

CENTRAL ADVISORY COUNCIL FOR EDUCATION. (1960). "15 to 18". Vol. II. London: H.M.S.O.

CHETWYND, H.R. (1960). "Comprehensive School—the Story of Woodberry Down". London: Routledge and Kegan Paul.

COHEN, P.C. (1968). "Modern Social Theory". London: Heinemann.

COLEMAN, J.S. (1961). "The Adolescent Society". London: Collier Macmillan.

CONNOLLY, T.G. & SLUCKIN, W. (1962). "Statistics for the Social Sciences". London: Cleaver-Hume Press.

CORWIN, R.G. (1967). Education and the sociology of complex organisations. In D.A. Hansen & J.E. Gerstl. (Eds.), "On Education: Sociological Perspectives". London: Wiley.

COSIN, B.R., DALE, I.R., ESLAND, G.M. & SWIFT, D.F. (1971). "School and Society: A Sociological Reader". London: Routledge and Kegan Paul.

COWELL, C.C. (1973). The contribution of physical activity to social development. In J.A. Mangan (Ed.). "Physical Education and Sport: Sociological and Cultural Perspectives". Oxford: Blackwell.

CRATTY, B.J. (1967). "Social Dimensions of Physical Activity". New Jersey: Prentice Hall.

CRUNDEN, C.C. (1970). Sport and social background: a study of 13 and 15 year old children. *Bull. of Phys. Educ.*, 8, 36-40.

DALE, R.R. (1974). "Mixed or Single-Sex School". London: Routledge and Kegan Paul.

DAWE, E.A. (1971). The two sociologies. In K. Thompson & J. Tunstall. (Eds.). "Sociological Perspectives". Harmondsworth: Penguin.

DEUTSCH, M. (1968). The effects of co-operation and competition upon group process. In D. Cartwright & A. Zander (Eds.). "Group Dynamics". London: Tavistock Publications.

DUMAZEDIER, J. (1967). "Toward a Society of Leisure". London: Collier-Macmillan.

DUNNING, E. (Ed.). (1971). "The Sociology of Sport". London: Cass.

EGGLESTON, S.J. (1967). "The Social Context of the School". London: Routledge and Kegan Paul.

ELIAS, N. & DUNNING, E. (1966). Dynamics of group sport with special reference to football., *B.J. Sociol.*, 14, 388-402.

EMMETT, I. (1971). "Youth and Leisure in an Urban Sprawl". Manchester: University Press.

EVANS, K.M. (1962). "Sociometry and Education". London: Routledge and Kegan Paul.

EVETTS, J. (1973). "The Sociology of Educational Ideas". London: Routledge and Kegan Paul.

FLOUD, J. (1950). Educational opportunity and social mobility. London: The Yearbook of Education.

FLOUD, J. (1967). The sociology of education. In A.T. Welford, M. Argyle, D.V. Glass & J.N. Morris. (Eds.). "Society: Problems and Methods of Study". London: Routledge and Kegan Paul.

FLOUD, J., HALSEY, A.H. & MARTIN, I. (1956). "Social Class and Educational Opportunity". London: Heinemann.

FORD, J. (1969). "Social Class and the Comprehensive School". London: Routledge and Kegan Paul.

FRANKENBERG, R. (1966). "Communities in Britain". Harmondsworth: Penguin.

GIBB, C.A. (1969). "Leadership". Harmondsworth: Penguin.

GLASS, D.V. (Ed.). (1954). "Social Mobility in Britain". London: Routledge and Kegan Paul.

GOFFMAN, E. (1961). "Encounters". New York: Bobbs-Merrill.

GORDON, C.W. (1957). "The Social System of the High School". New York: The Free Press.

GROSS, N. & HERRIOTT, R.W. (1965). "Staff Leadership in Public Schools". London: Wiley.

GROSS, N. & FISHMAN, J.A. (1968). The management of educational establishments. In P.F. Lazarsfeld. (Ed.). "The Uses of Sociology". London: Weidenfeld and Nicolson.

GROSS, N., MASON, W. S. & MCEACHEARN, A.W. (1958). "Explorations in Role Analysis". London: Wiley.

GRUSKY, O. (1969). The effects of formal structure on managerial recruitment: a study of baseball organisation. In J.W. Loy & G.S. Kenyon. (Eds.). "Sport, Culture and Society". London: Collier-Macmillan.

HALSEY, A.H., FLOUD, J. & ANDERSON, C.A. (1961). "Education, Economy and Society". London: Collier-Macmillan.

HARGREAVES, D.H. (1967). "Social Relations in a Secondary School". London: Routledge and Kegan Paul.

HARGREAVES, D.H. (1972). "Interpersonal Relations and Education". London: Routledge and Kegan Paul.

HIRST, P.H. (1966). Educational theory. In J.W. Tibble. (Ed.). "The Study of Education". London: Routledge and Kegan Paul.

HOCH, P. (1974). "The Newspaper Game". London: Calder and Boyars.

HOPPER, E. (Ed.). "Readings in the Theory of Educational Systems". London: Hutchinson.

HOYLE, E. (1969). "The Role of the Teacher". London: Routledge and Kegan Paul.

HOYLE, E. (1973). The study of schools as organisations. In H.J. Butcher & H.B. Pont. (Eds.). "Educational Research in Britain". London: University Press.

JACKSON, P.W. (1968). "Life in Classrooms". London: Holt, Rinehart and Winston.

JACKSON, B. & MARSDEN, D. (1966). "Education and the Working Class". Harmondsworth: Penguin.

JEPHCOTT, P. (1967). "Time of One's Own". Edinburgh: Oliver and Boyd.

KANE, J. (1974). "Physical Education in Secondary Schools". London: Macmillan.

KATZ, E. & LAZARSFELD, P.F. (1964). "Personal Influence". New York: The Free Press.

KENYON, G.S. (1969). A sociology of sport: on becoming a sub-discipline. In R. Brown & B.J. Cratty. (Eds.). "New Perspectives of Man in Action". New Jersey: Prentice-Hall.

KENYON, G.S. & LOY, J.W. (1969). Toward a sociology of sport. In J.W. Loy & G.S. Kenyon. (Eds.). "Sport, Culture and Society". London: Collier-Macmillan.

KEOGH, J. (1962). Extreme attitudes towards physical education. Res. Quart., 34, 27-33.

KING, R. (1969). "Values and Involvement in a Grammar School." London: Routledge and Kegan Paul.

KING, R. (1973). "School Organisation and Pupil Involvement: A Study of Secondary Schools". London: Routledge and Kegan Paul.

KLEIN, M. & CHRISTIANSEN, G. (1969). Group composition, group structure and group effectiveness of basketball teams. In J.W. Loy & G.S. Kenyon. (Eds.). "Sport, Culture and Society". London: Collier-Macmillan.

KLEIN, J. (1965). "Samples from English Cultures". Vol. 1. London: Routledge and Kegan Paul.

LACEY, C. (1970). "Hightown Grammar: the School as a Social System". Manchester: University Press.

LAMBERT, R. (1967). The public schools: a sociological introduction. In G. Kalton (Ed.). "The Public Schools: A Factual Survey". London: Longmans.

LAMBERT, L. & MILLHAM, S. (1974). "The Hothouse Society". London: Pelican.

LAWTON, D. (1975). "Class, Culture and the Curriculum". London: Routledge and Kegan Paul.

LEIGH, J. (1971). "Young People and Leisure". London: Routledge and Kegan Paul.

LENK, H. (1969). Top performance despite internal conflict. In J.W. Loy & G.S. Kenyon. (Eds.). "Sport, Culture and Society". London: Collier-Macmillan.

LIPPITT, R. & WHITE, R.K. (1952). An experimental study of leadership and group life. In G.E. Swanson, T.M. Newcomb & E.L. Hartley (Eds.). "Readings in Social Psychology". New York: Holt, Rinehart and Winston.

LOVEDAY, R. (1971). "A First Course in Statistics". Cambridge: University Press.

LOY, J.W. (1969). The nature of sport: a definitional effort. In J.W. Loy & G.S. Kenyon. (Eds.). "Sport, Culture and Society". London: Collier-Macmillan.

LOY, J.W. & KENYON, G.S. (Eds.). (1969). "Sport, Culture and Society". London: Collier-Macmillan.

LUSCHEN, G. (Ed.). (1970). "The Cross-Cultural Analysis of Sport and Games". Illinois: Stipes.

MCINTOSH, P.C. (1963). "Sport in Society". London: Watts.

MCINTOSH, P.C. (1966). Mental ability and success in sport. Res. in Phys. Educ., 1, 20-27.

MCLUHAN, M.M. (1971). "Understanding, Media: The Extension of Man". London: Sphere Books

MCQUAIL, D. (1969). "Toward a Sociology of Mass Communications". London: Collier-Macmillan.

MADGE, J. (1953). "The Tools of Social Science". London: Longmans.

MANGAN, J.A. (1973). Some sociological concomitants of secondary school physical education. In J.A. Mangan (Ed.). "Physical Education and Sport: Sociological and Cultural Perspectives". Oxford: Blackwell.

MANGAN, J.A. (Ed.). (1973). "Physical Education and Sport: Sociological and Cultural Perspectives". Oxford: Blackwell.

MAULDON, E. (1973). Communication through movement. In J.D. Brooke and H.T.A. Whiting. (Eds.). "Human Movement—A Field of Study". London: Kimpton.

MAYS, J.B. (1961). "Education and the Urban Child". Liverpool: University Press.

MERRILL, F.E. (1965). "Society and Culture". London: Prentice Hall.

MILLER, T.W.G. (1961). "Values in the Comprehensive School". Edinburgh: Oliver and Boyd.

MILLS, T.M. (1967). "The Sociology of Small Groups". London: Prentice Hall.

MONKS, T.G. (Ed.). (1970). "Comprehensive Education in Action". Slough: N.F.E.R.

MORENO, J.L. (1933). Psychological organisation of groups in the community. Year Book of Mental Deficiency. Boston.

MORONEY, M.J. (1951). "Facts from Figures". Harmondsworth: Penguin.

MORTON-WILLIAMS, R. & FINCH, S. (1968). "Schools Council Enquiry 1: Young School Leavers". London: H.M.S.O.

MOSER, C.A. & KALTON, G. (1973). "Survey Methods in Social Investigation". London: Heinemann.

MUSGRAVE, P.W. (1968). "The School as an Organisation". London: Macmillan.

NADEL, S.F. (1965). "The Theory of Social Structure". London: Cohen and West.

NORTHWAY, M.L. (1959). "A Primer of Sociometry". Toronto: University Press.

NORTHWAY, M.L. (1951). A note on the use of target sociograms. Sociometry, 14, 235-236.

OPPENHEIM, A.N. (1966). "Questionnaire Design and Attitude Measurement". London: Heinemann.

PARKER, S.R. (1972). "The Future of Work and Leisure". London: Paladin.

PARSONS, T. (1969). The school class as a social system. In A.H. Halsey, J. Floud, & C.A. Anderson (Ed.). "Education, Economy and Society". London: Collier-Macmillan.

PARTRIDGE, J. (1966). "Life in a Secondary Modern School". Harmondsworth: Penguin.

ROBERTS, K. (1970). "Leisure". London: Longman.

ROCHE, A.G. (1965). Attitude testing in physical education with 14-15 year old boys. Carnegie College of Physical Education: Research Papers in Physical Education, 1, 29-37.

ROSS, J.M., BUNTON, W.J., EVISON, P. & ROBERTSON, T.S. (1972). "A Critical Appraisal of Comprehensive Education". Slough: N.F.E.R.

SAGE, G.H. (Ed.). (1970). "Sport and American Society: Selected Readings". London: Addison-Wesley.

SAUNDERS, C. (1974). An investigation of secondary school children's attitude to physical education in school. New University of Ulster: Dip. Adv. St. of Educ.

SAUNDERS, E.D. (1971). Aspects of change and physical education in the social system of the school. *Scottish Bull. of Phys. Educ.* **8**, 4.

SAUNDERS, E.D. (1973). Sociological orientation to the study of physical education. In J.A. Mangan (Ed.). "Physical Education and Sport: Sociological and Cultural Perspectives." Oxford: Blackwell.

SAUNDERS, E.D. (1974). Theory and practice in physical education. *Bull. of Phys. Educ.*, **10**, 13-21.

SAUNDERS, E.D. & WITHERINGTON, K.S. (1970). Extra-curricular physical activities in secondary schools. *B.J. Phys. Educ.*, **1**, 10-14.

SELLITZ, D., JAHODA, M., DEUTSCH, M. & COOK, S.W. (1966). "Research Methods in Social Research". London: Methuen.

SHIPMAN, M.D. (1968). "Sociology of the School". London: Longmans.

SILLITOE, K.K. (1969). "Planning for Leisure". London: H.M.S.O.

SILVERMAN, D., (1971). "The Theory of Organisation". London: Heinemann.

SMIGEL, E.D. (Ed.). (1963). "Work and Leisure". New Haven: College and University Press.

SMITH, M.A., PARKER, S. & SMITH, C.S. (Eds.). (1973). "Leisure and Society in Britain". London: Lane.

SPINLEY, B.W. (1953). "The Deprived and the Privileged". London: Routledge and Kegan Paul.

STACEY, M. (1969). "Methods of Social Research". London: Pergamon.

START, K.B. (1961). The relationship between games performance of the grammar school boy and his intelligence and streaming. *B.J. Educ. Psychol.*, **31**, 208-211.

START, K.B. (1967). Substitution of games performance as a means of achieving status amongst secondary school boys. *B.J. Sociol.*, **17**, 300-305.

STEVENS, F. (1971). "The Living Tradition". London: Hutchinson.

SWIFT, D.F. (1969). "The Sociology of Education". London: Routledge and Kegan Paul.

TAYLOR, W. (1961). "The Secondary Modern School". London: Faber.

TAYLOR, W. (1966). The sociology of education. In J.W. Tibble (Ed.). "The Study of Education". London: Routledge and Kegan Paul.

THE SCHOOL AND SOCIETY COURSE TEAM. (1971). The construction of reality. In "School and Society, Units 1 and 2". Bletchley: The Open University Press.

WAKEFORD, J. (1969). "The Cloistered Elite". London: Macmillan.

WARREN, N. & JAHODA, M. (1973). (Eds.). "Attitudes". Harmondsworth: Penguin.

WALLER, W. (1967). "The Sociology of Teaching". London: Wiley.

WARD, F., HARDMAN, K. & ALMOND, L. (1968). Investigations into the problem of participation and attitudes to physical activity of 11-18 year old boys. *Research in Physical Education*, **1**, 18-26.

WHITE, G.B. (1966). A Sociometric Investigation of the Effects of Three Different Types of Indoor Lesson in Physical Education. Carnegie College of Physical Education: *Research Papers in Physical Education*, **2**, 47-53.

WHITE, G.B., WHITELEY, G., VENTRE, A.G.L. & MASON, M.G. (1965). Attitude to athletics of second and fourth year boys in secondary schools. Carnegie College of Physical Education: *Research Papers in Physical Education*, **1**, 51-54.

WILKINSON, R.H. (1964). "The Prefects. British Leadership and the Public School Tradition". Oxford: University Press.

WORSLEY, P. (1970). "Introducing Sociology". Harmondsworth: Penguin.

Index

Index

Middle class   17, 29, 36
Mobility   19

N
Need(s)   29
Negotiation   31, 32
Newsom Report   28
Newspaper   45
Norm(s)   19, 50, 54, 59
Normative approach   13, 15, 20

O
Open University   18

P
Personality   26, 31, 70, 79
Perspective   13
Philosophy   78
Physical education   11, 13, 15, 16, 17, 18, 19, 20,
   26, 27, 28, 32, 36, 37, 39, 44, 50, 51, 53, 54, 64,
   65, 66, 68, 69, 71, 72, 78, 90
Physiology   11, 16
Public school   46

Q
Questionnaire   66, 67, 69, 70, 71, 73

R
Race   44
Recreation   12, 13, 20, 36, 40, 44, 47, 50, 51, 52, 70
Rejection   54
Relationship(s)   16, 17, 28, 32, 60, 78
Research   12, 19, 64
Role, pupil/teacher   28, 29, 79, 80, 81

S
School   11, 16, 18, 31, 33, 34, 36, 44, 50, 64, 65, 68,
   78
Schools Council   18

Secondary modern school   16, 27, 36, 65, 66
Sex   37, 40, 44, 51
Social change   12, 40
   class   12, 16, 18, 36, 37, 44
   control   12, 27, 31
   development   16
   mobility   12, 17
   order   14, 44
   philosophy   14
   pressure   40
   stratification   17
   system   14, 19
Socialization   12, 27
Society   19, 20, 26, 27, 31, 44, 89
Sociology   10, 13, 14, 15, 16, 17, 19, 20, 26, 27, 53,
   65
Sociogram   53, 54, 55, 57
Sociomatrix   53, 54
Sociometric choice   53
   status   54, 55
   test   54, 55
Specialist   67
Sport   11, 13, 17, 20, 39, 44, 45, 47
Star, definition of   57
Statistics   20
Status   28
Stratification   19
Streams   18, 28, 70
Systems approach   14, 27, 31
Survey   16, 36, 39

T
Teachers   16, 21, 27, 28, 31, 32, 66, 69, 80
Technical school   16, 36
Theory   20, 64, 65

V
Values   13, 17, 19, 26, 27, 28, 31
Vertigo   70

W
Working class   36